Connecticut Decoys

Connecticut Decoys

Carvers and Gunners

By Henry C. Chitwood
with Thomas C. Marshall and Doug Knight

Schiffer Publishing Ltd

West Chester, Pennsylvania 19380

Title page: Tom Marshall and Miley Bull off Stratford.

Library of Congress Catalog Number: 86-61703.

Printed in the United States of America.
ISBN: 0-88740-104-X
Published by Schiffer Publishing Ltd.
1469 Morstein Road, West Chester, Pennsylvania 19380

This book may be purchased from the publisher.
Please include $2.00 postage.
Try your bookstore first.

Dedication

To Tom Marshall

Thoughts from a Friend

Of America's heritage the wildfowl decoy is one of the last to be recognized as a work of art as well as a hunting device. Thomas C. Marshall was one of the first sportsmen to recognize this fact. His happy hunting ground was Connecticut where the Housatonic River flows into Long Island Sound, the home of the Stratford carvers.

One day Tom took me to Stratford to the house where Albert Laing had lived. He told me about Shang Wheeler and Benjamin Holmes. At his own home he showed me decoys carved by the "Big Three". He gave me a working decoy, a black duck carved by Wheeler.

Throughout the years the home of Tom and Betty has been a mecca for collectors and writers. Always he shared his knowledge, his time, his love. His notes and records were made available to me and to the author of this new definitive book on Connecticut decoys.

Tom worked with "Ducks Unlimited", the National Sportsman's Show, and many decoy carving contests to help the promotion and appreciation of the decoy. Thank you Tom, as fine and sweet and knowledgeable a friend as the decoys and I will ever know.

Adele Earnest

Acknowledgments

This book had its beginning in initial research done by Thomas C. Marshall. Many of the facts were taken from his biographical records on Albert Laing and Benjamin Holmes, and of later Stratford decoy makers he had known. He pointed the way to sources of further information. The older photographs of Stratford people and hunting scenes were also furnished by Marshall or Mrs. Marshall.

Most of the decoy photographs in the book were taken by Doug Knight who, at the same time, through taped conversations with their owners, acquired personal knowledge of some of the old time carvers.

Thanks go to the Shelburne Museum, Richard A. Bourne and Co., and William Doyle Galleries, who permitted their decoys to be photographed and furnished some photographs on request. Other auction houses that granted photographic permission were James D. Julia and Richard W. Oliver. Photographs were kindly supplied also by Julie and Michael Hall, Mr. and Mrs. Clune Walsh, Philip Morse, Louis MacDowell, Stephen O'Brien, and Ronald Swanson. Other photographs are from the collections of the Old Lighthouse Museum of Stonington, Mrs. A. C. Clayton, Les Collins, Donald Doyle, Tim Eastland, Joseph Filanowski, Ronald Frumkes, Edward Gessner, Kenneth Gleason, Alan Haid, Tod Lovell, Charles Mackall, Horace Merwin, Donal O'Brien, Peter Pasky, Kenneth Waite, and George Wilcox, as well as Thomas Marshall, Doug Knight, and the writer.

The research on Laing started with his Journal, owned by Thomas Marshall, and was followed by study of records of the Society of Friends, of New York, and other documents and by examination of decoys from several sources, a key group being one owned by Stephen O'Brien. The writer gives special thanks to Ronald Swanson, with whom he discussed the Laing mysteries and who gave reassuring support to the fresh conclusions reached from the research on Laing and Holmes.

Editorial assistance was supplied by Doug Knight. Others who read portions of the manuscript and offered constructive and helpful editorial suggestions were Alan Haid and especially Julia Chitwood.

Many facts were obtained directly from individuals mentioned in the text—gunners, carvers, and associates—who are living or have died within the past ten years. Among the many others who have provided facts or have been helpful in other ways are: Gunnar Anderson, Mrs. Willard Baldwin, Peter Baronoski, Miley Bull, Roy Bull, Mrs. William Bedell, George Campbell, Dr. William Caragol, Mr. and Mrs. Carleton Clark, Mrs. Reginald Culver, John DeCesare, Kirkley Dows, Robert Foreman, Dr. Nathan Friedman, Chet Gillis, Ted Harmon, Cary Hunt, Peter Lanier, Frank Lyke, Ada Mae Maniatis, John Mayer, Carmen Mulliken, Daniel O'Brien, Robert Reineck, Robert Shaw, Mrs. Paul Sperry, Mrs. James Tremaine, Mitchell Van Winkle, William Varady, Tilford Wade, and William Walsh.

May 1987 Henry Chitwood

Foreword

Connecticut was the home of men who deserve much credit for the current interest in decoys. Albert Laing and Benjamin Holmes produced quality decoys in the nineteenth century and set a high standard for their followers. Shang Wheeler led the trend, with delicately sculptured and elaborately painted birds, toward decorative carving. He, along with Joel Barber by his collecting and writing, and Tom Marshall through the national carving contests, fostered the artistic appreciation of decoys.

Over the past forty years the interest in collecting "decoys" has increased tremendously and has created a great demand for bird carvings in general, including purely decorative and finely carved and feathered examples, as well as copies made to simulate old working birds. Though many of these carvings have artistic merit, this book focuses solely on the working decoys carved by the old time makers.

The aims of this book are, by description and photograph:

a) to show the history of development of styles of Connecticut decoys and their regional differences,

b) to point out the influence of major makers upon their contemporaries and successors, and the master-follower relationships that occurred,

c) to identify as many worthwhile carvers as possible, and to indicate the features of each individual's work, with dates when known, to aid the reader in identification, and

d) to provide biographical and historical material on important makers of Connecticut decoys and the gunners who used them.

Species of ducks and their decoys are generally identified in the text by their common names, such as black duck, mallard, and pintail. In some cases, names are shortened or the vernacular of the hunter is used. The terms, broadbill, bluebill, and scaup, are used for both lesser scaup and greater scaup. Red-breasted merganser is shortened to merganser or sheldrake. Whistler is synonymous with goldeneye, and black ducks are simply blacks.

Contents

Opposite page:
Bill Bedell and Lou Rathmell with "Jiggs" on Bedell's boat, "Ideal."

Table of Carvers

The following table lists most of the known Connecticut decoy makers who were active before 1950. The vital dates of many are not known, but when given, are mostly from town records and believed to be correct. Less accuracy is claimed for the carving periods and the numbers of decoys made. In some cases, they are just guesses that hopefully approximate the facts.

Carver	Dates	Location	Carving Period	Estimated Total Made	Description-Known Species
ADAMS, Franklin W.	c. 1902-	Essex	1930s		wood and cork, scaup and black duck
BALDWIN, Arthur		Stratford	1880s		Broadbill
BALDWIN, Willard C.	1890-1979	Stratford	1910-1975	250-300	Black, scaup, goldeneye, and decoratives
BANNING, Frank	-1970	Hadlyme/Noank	1930s	30-40	Scaup, merganser
BANNING, Herbert	-c. 1960	Old Lyme	1920s		Black
BARBER, Joel	1876-1952	N. Y./Wilton	1930s	50	Black, mallard, scaup, redhead, goldeneye
BEDELL, William E. III	1909-1966	Stratford	1933	25	Black only
BENTLEY, William C.	1909-1980	Stratford	1940	15	Black only
BLISS, Roswell E.	1887-1967	Stratford	1901-1967	1000+	Nearly all species
BRADLEY, Robert S.	1874-1969	Branford	1904		Scaup
BREWSTER, Swan	1899-pres	Stratford/N. Y.	1930-pres		Black, scaup, teal
BREIT, William Russell	1893-1955	Stratford	c. 1940	12	Black
BROWN, James Halstead	1890-1974	Noank	1910-1945	100+	Shelldrake, broadbill, bufflehead
BUCKINGHAM		Essex	1880s		
BULL, Milan John	1914-1980	Milford	1970s		Cork black
CAMPBELL, Isaac	1840-	Norwalk	1860s		Shore birds
CHACE, Arthur	-pres	Fairfield		120	Silhouettes
CLAYTON, Arthur	1911-1974	Fairfield	late 1930s, 40s	25-30	Black, scaup
COATES, Albert E.	1868-1963	Branford	turn of the century		Scaup
COATES, Lewis W.	1911-1965	Branford	early 1930s		Scaup
COLLINS, Samuel, Sr.	c. 1830-	Essex			Black, merganser
COLLINS, Samuel, Jr.	1854-1948	Essex	1875-1930		Black, scaup, bufflehead, American merganer
COMSTOCK, George		Essex			
COYKENDALL, Ralf, Sr.	1892-1968	Weston	1930-1968	200+	Black, mallard, widgeon, canvasback, redhead
CULVER, Irving	1906-1972	Stratford	1920s-30s		Black
CULVER, Reginald I.	1897-1975	Stratford	1910-1965	150	Black, broadbill
CULVER, Robert	1873-1958	Stratford	c. 1900		Black
DISBROW, Charles R.	1885-1955	Stratford	1910-1955	75	Black
DUDKOWSKI, Edmund	1905-1977	Jewett City	1930s	30+	Black, mallard
EWEN, John		West Hartford			Black
FAIRBANKS, Philip, Sr.		Old Saybrook			
FAIRBANKS, Philip, Jr.		Old Saybrook			
GANUNG, Lon	1883-1972	West Haven	1910-1960		Black, mallard
GLADDING, Coit P.	1844-1917	Essex			
GORDEAUX, Wesley		Glastonbury			
HALL, Aaron		Haddam Meadows	c. 1930		Black
HANFORD, John	1840-1931	Stratford	c. 1885		Black

Carver	Dates	Location	Carving Period	Estimated Total Made	Description-Known Species
HARLOW, Frank	1873-1968	Branford	c. 1900		Shore birds
HARRIS, Marion	1914-pres	Old Saybrook	1945-1980		Painted only
HARRIS, Richard	1910-1980	Old Saybrook	1942-1980		Many species
HOADLEY, Howard	1888-1937	Milford	1920-1935		Black, scaup
HOLMES, Benjamin	1843-1912	Stratford	1870-1912	1000+	Black, scaup, goldeneye, redhead, canvasback, merganser
HUBBELL, Walter S.	1880-1945	Stratford	1900-1930		Black
HUNT, Samuel	-1950	Essex	1920-1930		Black, scaup
HUNTER, Robert	1899-1983	Southport	1960-1980	c. 40	Black, scaup
HURLBURT, James G.		Essex	1900-1910		Goldeneye
HYDE, Howard	1916-pres	Stratford	1936-1950	50-60	Black, mallard, scaup
KOEHLER, Harold		New Milford			Cork decoys
LAING, Albert D.	1811-1886	Stratford	1835-1860	300	Black, scaup, goldeneye, pintail, canvasback, brant, swan
LaPLACE, Oliver	1901-pres	Essex	1920-pres	500+	Black, mallard, scaup, canvasback
LARSON, "Swede"		Saybrook			Cork black
LATTIN, William V.	-1934	Stratford	1890s		Black, broadbill
MARSHALL, Thomas C.	1903-1983	Fairfield	1950-60s	100+	Most common species
MERWIN, Horace	1888-1947	Southport	1940-45	c. 20	Black, mallard, scaup, others
MILES, Jimmy Lew		Stratford			Scaup
MULLIKEN, Edward	1896-1964	Old Saybrook	1920-1957	1000s	Most species
PALMER, Nathaniel B.	1799-18	Stonington	c 1820-1850		Shore birds, silhouettes
PECK, Kenneth	1887-1961	Stratford	1933	30-40	Black
PHELPS, Judy	-1952	Essex	1920-1930s	500+	Black, decoratives
PRATT, Ned	c 1885-1970	Essex	1900-1950		Black
RATHMELL, Louis	1898-1974	Danbury	1920-1960	50+	Black, mallard, redhead, teal, bufflehead
ROMER, Byron	1859-1917	Stratford			Scaup, goldeneye
ROSS, Harry	1914-pres	Old Saybrook	1926-pres	1000	Most North American species
SANFORD, Al		Saugatuck	1880s		
SELLECK, J. W.		South Norwalk	1870s-80s		Scaup
SMITH, Captain	-1960	Noank			Merganser
SMITH, Cassius	1847-1907	Milford	late 1880s		Scaup, goldeneye
SMITH, George T.	1824-1894	Milford	mid 1800s		
SPERRY, Paul A.	1895-1982	New Haven	1920s		Black, mallard, scaup, canvasback, golden-eye
STANNARD, William Henry	1874-1931	Branford	1900-1930		Scaup
STOCKMAN, Edward		Oxford			
THOMAS, Steve	1865-1938	East Haven	1890-1920	100s	Black, scaup
TOOKER, Bertram		Essex			Scaup
VARADY, Michael		Byram	1930s-40s	100	Scaup, old squaw
WARNER, Rastus		Joshuatown			Black, goldeneye, merganser
WEBBER, William	c. 1969	Essex			
WELLER, Bruce H.	1848-1925	Stratford	1870-1900		Black
WELLES, Charles ("Chick")		Stratford			Scaup
WELLES, Charles Ralph	1895-1979	Stratford	1916-1976	200	Black, mallard, scaup, teal, canvasback
WHEELER, Charles E.	1872-1949	Stratford	1890-1948	500-600	Many species, workers and decoratives
WICKS, Charles D.	1860-1921	Stratford			
WILCOX, Moses, H.	1858-1963!	Mystic	late 19th century		Black-covered with duck skins, mergansers

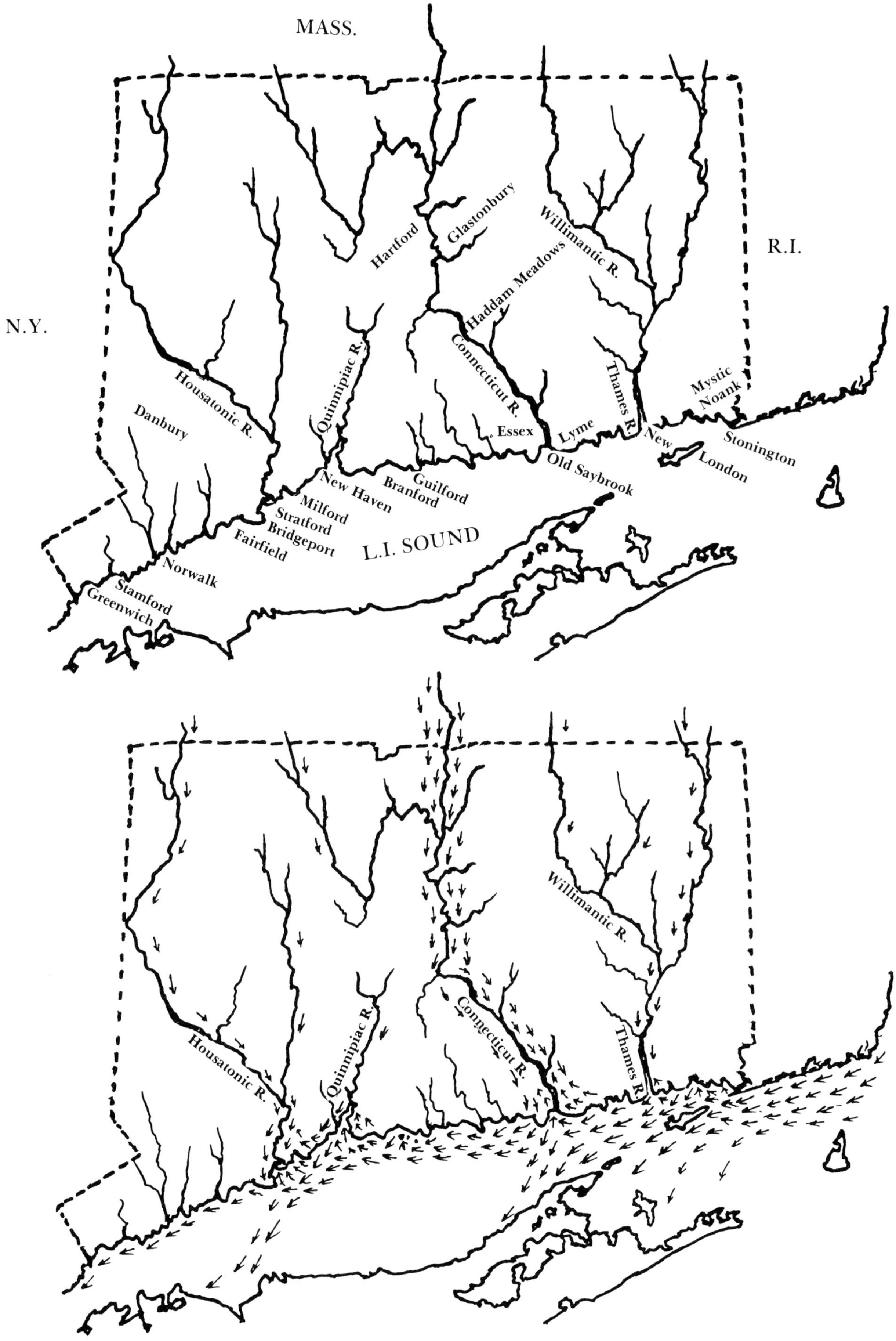

FALL MIGRATION ROUTES THROUGH CONNECTICUT

I.
Duck Hunting in Connecticut

The migratory waterfowl that breed in eastern Canada have, for millennia, travelled through Connecticut, dropping in along the way for food and rest. Opportunities for both are found in the myriad of ponds and lakes across the state, and in the coves and inlets along the coast. Many of the migrants pick up the mighty Connecticut River near its source and follow it along the New Hampshire-Vermont border, through Massachusetts into Connecticut. Others come by the saltwater route, from the Maritime Provinces, down the coast of Maine, Massachusetts, and Rhode Island.

When ducks that have taken the overland or freshwater route reach Long Island Sound, some continue across the water to Long Island, but many veer southwestward, feeding in the estuaries and marshes along the Connecticut coast. Here these streams of surface feeders—the teal, black ducks, widgeon and others—meet the sea-loving coastal ducks. Groups from both directions move down the coastline together, sharing the same feeding grounds. Some of the scaup, goldeneys, and other diving ducks join up via the Connecticut River, but most of them, and all of the sea ducks, like the scoters and old squaws, come by the sea route.

Ducks are taken throughout Connecticut during the fall and winter migration, but gunning is concentrated where the big congregations of ducks are found—in the Connecticut River and along the coast, near the mouths of the Thames, Connecticut, Quinnipiac, and Housatonic Rivers and in the marshy and rugged inlets and areas surrounding Connecticut's many small islands.

The numbers of waterfowl following the different flight paths have varied over the years. Tom Marshall observed that, at the time he arrived in Connecticut in the mid-twenties, the Connecticut River was a major flyway. "More ducks came down (the river) and the hunting was better here than anywhere else in the state. For the next twenty or thirty years the Connecticut River got worse, while the Housatonic River and the Norwalk Islands got better."

Flights of a century ago that were reported to number in the hundreds of thousands are no longer seen. The general trend has been toward fewer migrating ducks, resulting partly from hunting pressure but more from destruction of nesting grounds. In spite of lower bag limits, the decrease in the number of black ducks over the past ten years has been alarming.

Before the 1940's, migrating Canada geese made few stops in Connecticut, and mallards were uncommon as either residents or migrants. Willard Baldwin, a seasoned Stratford gunner, once commented that when he shot his first mallard, probably about 1925, he "didn't know what it was." The only ducks that nested in the State were wood ducks and black ducks. Hunters distinguish the local black ducks, with brownish-colored legs from the more highly prized Canadian-bred strain, the "red-leggers."

We now have two additional locally nesting species, the Canada goose and mallard. Both have extended their nesting range, the geese southward from Canada and mallards eastward and southward. Many are year-round residents.

The population of mallards and geese was augmented by a state-operated program of raising and releasing birds in the 1940's. Since both species are easily domesticated, the descendants of the state-raised stock retain their semi-domestic habits and, where not molested, have become abundant. Canada geese are now considered a nuisance in public parks and golf courses and lawns of suburban sections of Connecticut and neighboring states.

The State's attempt at stocking widgeon and pintails did not succeed in noticeably increasing their numbers locally. Instead of taking up residence, those that survived apparently migrated with the wild flocks, nesting farther north.

II.
The Housatonic River Area

STRATFORD

The region around the mouth of the Housatonic River was the greatest gunning area in Connecticut and the one where its most famous decoy makers lived. The town of Stratford, settled in 1639, lies on the right-hand or west bank of the river, and Milford, settled at the same time, is on the east bank. The marshes and shoal waters of the area made it a favorite feeding ground for migrating waterfowl.

Extending from the Milford side is a marshland known as Knell's Island, acquired by Nicholas Knell about 1650. At the time of Albert Laing it was a distinct island of only ten acres. Over the years, as a result of building a dam and breakwater, and through the action of floods and hurricanes, silting has increased the marsh to over 600 acres. Charles Island, which is a higher and drier island of about twelve acres, is in Long Island Sound, separated from the mainland of Milford by a half-mile of very shallow water.

The most common decoys of the Housatonic region are scaup and black ducks, followed by goldeneyes. Among the older decoys, old squaws are next in abundance, indicating that this species was in the past a more common quarry than today. The proportion of scoters is also higher among the older decoys. Decoys of other species—merganser, canvas-back, ruddy duck, and mallard—are rare and were seldom used before 1920. The earliest Canada goose decoys to survive in any quantity were made by Shang Wheeler and Roswell Bliss, and a few brant have been attributed to Ben Holmes.

The oldest decoys known to have been used in the Housatonic gunning waters vary considerably in shape. They were made by independently-minded individuals for their own use, seemingly uninfluenced by styles of contemporaries. Most are unimpressive solid blocks, inferior to the later ones used in the area, but some have folk art appeal. The names of their creators are lost to history.

The early gunners, many of them market hunters, were all intent on high kills with minimum effort and were not concerned with our modern-day concept of sportsmanship. Birds were shot on the water and the decoys sitting among the quarry received lots of shot damage. This, combined with the deleterious effect of salt water on the paint, necessitated frequent refurbishing. Reheading, and repainting were all parts of the job of keeping a decoy in proper working condition. Decoys were used for many years and passed through the hands of successive owners, some of whom made alterations, adding glass eyes, changing the ballast weight, and reshaping or replacing a head in attempts to improve the appearance or performance. These modifications have contributed to the difficulty of positive identification and of determining to what degree a decoy is "original."

A revolution in decoy making occurred with the arrival of Albert Laing in Stratford in 1863. He introduced a hollow decoy with a distinctive and attractive appearance. The features, which included a high breast, rounded lines, and a paddle-like tail, were adopted by contemporary gunners and by the professional decoy maker, Benjamin Holmes. Both Laing and Holmes were imitated by Reginald Culver, Willard Baldwin, Ralph Welles, and others—even Shang Wheeler. But Wheeler was an artist and worked also from natural models. He varied the head positions and body design, and his decoys became famous for their lifelike appearance. He had a host of followers, the most prominent of whom was Roswell Bliss, who made decoys as a profession and who worked with Wheeler. The influence of Laing, Holmes, and Wheeler was so strong that most decoys from the region are easily recognized by style as of the "Stratford School."

The upward bow of the breast, combined with the balancing action of weight placed toward the rear, made the decoy ride over the waves with minimum downward drag and held it level over a wide range of currents.

Stratford decoys as a group contain an unusually large number whose attribution is uncertain and on which recognized experts disagree or have no opinion. Their history was seldom passed from one owner to the next. Most of the decoys of Albert Laing and Ben Holmes are readily identified, but positive identification of others made before 1900 is difficult.

Decoys by the better known laters carvers, such as Wheeler, Bliss, Baldwin, Welles, and Culver, are usually easily recognized, but many by lesser known and unknown makers are unattributed. Identification of twentieth century decoys is complicated by the fact that many were made by a joint effort of two individuals, and others were made up originally from parts of different origin. Heads were sold by Culver and the Wildfowler Company, and com-

Knell's Island facing north. As it appeared in 1940.

Typical layout of decoys on trawls, at mouth of the Housatonic River.

Tom Marshall in old scull and layout boat at the mouth of the Housatonic River. Note plug in scull hole.

mercial lathe operators turned out heads and bodies that were used by different men to construct their own decoys.

The identification problem is complicated by earlier publications that have given erroneous or questionable information. The chapter by Shang Wheeler in Eugene Connett's *Duck Shooting Along the Atlantic Tidewater* includes photographs of birds he credits to Albert Laing, Ben Holmes, Al Sanford of Saugatuck, and Francis Burritt and J. W. Selleck of Norwalk. While agreement between pictures and names of the first two seems to be correct, there is reason to question the attribution of the Burritt and Sanford birds, which, according to the dates give, were made when Wheeler was only a child.

Francis Burritt branded many of the birds he used, and most of those with his brand are now known to have been made by Laing or Holmes. It seems that Wheeler assigned the owners' names to the makers.

William Mackey's *American Bird Decoys* (1965) contains pictures that confuse the reader on Laing and Holmes. The birds he attributed to Holmes are actually Laing's. His misinformation has led to similar errors in later publications that have accepted Mackey's word. Mackey also incorrectly stated that decoys with the Culver brand were made by Holmes.

The practice of so many Stratford decoy makers of copying the work of predecessors and contemporaries has aggravated the problem of identification. At first glance so many of them look alike! Wheeler's activities in Stratford especially compounded the problem. He was an innovative and prolific artist who introduced a number of new designs. He was generous to fellow carvers, willingly giving patterns to all who requested them. He had a wide following of imitators, and some of them succeeded in producing decoys very difficult to distinguish from Wheeler's.

Another reason for inaccuracy in attribution results from the great disparity in monetary value of decoys by different makers. Culver's decoys have passed for Holmes' and frequently those by Bliss, Welles, or Rathmell have been misrepresented as Wheeler's.

The names of the Housatonic duck hunters who preceded Albert Laing have made no imprint on the history of the sport, but Shang Wheeler did name some who followed close behind, including Burritt, Sanford, and Selleck mentioned above, and also Captain Burr Smith and Captain George Allen of Saugatuck, Captain George Hine, Edward Laing and Ephriam Wakely of Stratford, Captain George Smith and Clark Baldwin of Milford, all of whom gunned through the 1870's and 80's. Later noted gunners known to Wheeler were Charles "Cappy" Wicks and Ash Bond of Stratford, Jimmy Lew Miles and Captain George Green of Milford, Dr. Len Sanford of New Haven, and others eastward to the

Rhode Island border. Among his own shooting companions in the early 1890's were Jim Pete, Herk Smith, Rad Smith, Anse Dart, and Charles ("Chick") Welles, some of whom may have made decoys. Welles was known to have made a few that were passed onto his son, Charles Ralph Welles, a prominent twentieth-century Stratford maker.

Decoys, like the birds they imitate, have mobility and are often found away from their birthplace. The source of decoys that possess distinctive features can usually be established, but for nondescript ones by unknown makers it is impossible. Some of those that do not match the characteristic style of the region where they are found are immigrants and others are the product of non-conformist carvers. Many such decoys of solid wood or cork are found in Stratford. A few of these, whose photographs are shown, are probably not "natives" and others were made by local carvers who lacked the classical education provided by Headmaster Laing's Stratford School.

ALBERT DAVIDS LAING (1811-1886)

Among collectors today, no name is held in higher esteem than Albert Laing. He is acclaimed as father of the Stratford School and recognized as one of the greatest decoy carvers who ever lived.

Albert Davids Laing was born in Rahway, New Jersey, in 1811 of Quaker parents, Hugh and Catherine Davids Laing. The family moved to New York City in 1820. Little is known of Laing's education or early life beyond what is stated in his shooting journal of four and a half years in New York and a diary he kept for three months in France. He probably lived in New York most of this time and worked for his father, a prosperous businessman who was a merchant, broker, and president of a fire insurance company.

Laing started shooting on the waters near New York City. He used a scull-boat from the Henry Robbins shipyard in Bridgeport, the town adjoining Stratford. The boat, that he named "Rose," was shipped to him on the "Commodore," a side-wheeler that ran from Shelton to New York City. Besides shooting from the "Rose," he sometimes hired batteries by the day.

He had become an avid duck hunter by the time he began his journal in October 1831 at the age of twenty. During the first fall season reported, he hunted nineteen times for a total kill of 187 waterfowl. On one December day in 1831, he bagged twelve blacks with one shot. The places mentioned in the record are Westchester Creek, Baxter Creek, Oyster Pond Point, the Narrows between City Island and Pelham, Eastchester Bay, Jerusalem South in Islip, Little Neck Bay, West Farms Bay, the Meadow, and the Dyke.

Albert Laing at about the time he moved to Stratford.

Laing's record summarized in the table below, covers two periods of gunning, from October 1831 to May 1836 in New York, and October 1863 to May 1871 in Connecticut. The latter period began when he bought a house and moved to Stratford, Connecticut, in 1863. The house, which still stands, is located on the Housatonic River shore opposite the Knell's Island marsh where he did much of his duck hunting. Other shooting spots he mentioned were Peck's Cove, Goose Island, Frash Pond, Coot Bar Basin, Quinby Neck, Old Field Cove, and Skate Bar.

His sporting activities slowly diminished and he apparently stopped hunting after seven years in Connecticut. His journal, expanded to include activities other than hunting, continued for another ten years, during which he devoted his time to agricultural projects, such as experimenting with new varieties of fruit and vegetables, raising game chickens, and breeding animals. He even tried raising silkworms and cultivating pearls. In spite of the detail devoted to these items, he never mentioned decoys.

Laing's gunning journal.

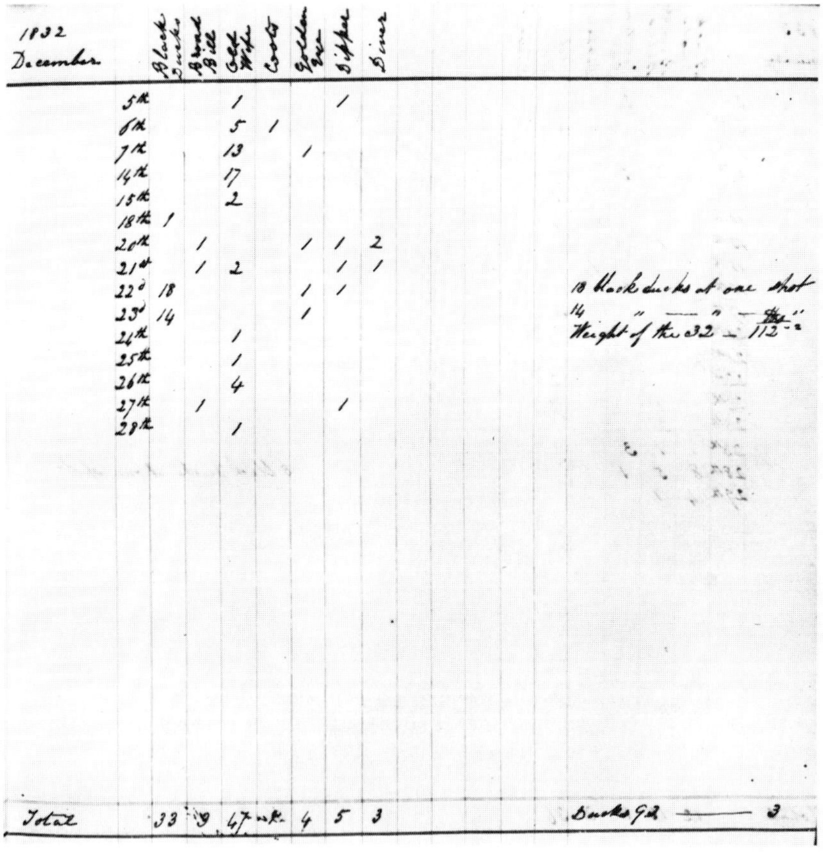

1832 December	Black Ducks	Broad Bill	Gold Wings	Coots	Golden Eye	Dipper	Divers
5th			1			1	
6th			5	1			
7th			13		1		
14th			17				
15th			2				
18th	1						
20th		1			1	1	2
21st		1	2			1	1
22d	18				1	1	
23d	14				1		
24th			1				
25th			1				
26th			4				
27th		1				1	
28th			1				
Total	33	3	47	[illegible]	4	5	3

18 black ducks at one shot
14 " — " — " "
Weight of the 32 = 112 lbs

Ducks 92 — 3

A page from Laing's journal.

Summary of Laing's Gunning Record

Species	*4 1/2 Years in New York* Number	Rank	*7 1/2 Years in Connecticut* Number	Rank
Broadbill	748	1	184	2
Old Squaw	545	2	183	3
Black Duck	488	3	23	4
Goldeneye	157	4	15	5
Bufflehead	155	5	6	
Coot (scoter)	133	6	569	1
Ruddy Duck	26		0	
Widgeon	7		15	5
Pintail	3		11	
Canvasback	1		0	
Sheldrake	11		13	
Mud Hen (common coot)	38		41	
Brant	6		1	
Goose	0		5	
Yellowlegs	29		14	
English Snipe (Wilson's)	55		0	
Rails	4		0	
Miscellaneous	38		5	
Totals	2443		1085	

From the preceding summary it can be seen that scoters accounted for more than half of Laing's waterfowl kill in Connecticut. He made both white-winged and surf scoter decoys, some of which were converted by later owners to black ducks. Broadbills, blacks, and goldeneyes, followed by canvasbacks, are his most commonly seen decoys. Next to scoters and broadbills, more old squaws were killed than any other species, yet no Laing old squaw decoys have been identified.

A study of Laing's journal, in relation to the decoys he left at the time of his death, raises a number of questions:

1. In view of the details given to most everyday activities, why did he never mention decoys or decoy making in his journal?
2. Since the journal does not indicate that he hunted canvasbacks, why did he make them?
3. Why did he leave no old squaws, though they ranked second in number killed in New York and third in Connecticut?
4. When did he make the decoys?

The twenty-seven year gap in the journal provides a basis for some of the answers. Two conclusions reached may be surprising to some: Laing's decoys were made before he moved to Connecticut, refuting the generally accepted view that he made them in Stratford. Ben Holmes did not originate the style of decoy with which he has been credited, but copied it directly from Laing.

There is no direct knowledge of Laing's life during the period of twenty-seven years from ages 25 to 52, except that he lived in France for two years, 1838-40. His decoys have been found in Virginia, Maryland, Massachusetts, Pennsylvania, and New York, suggesting that he maintained his interest in hunting and traveled extensively to the better gunning areas before settling in Connecticut. A black duck of solid wood bearing the unmistakable "LAING" brand was found in a Long Island antique shop. A souvenir of his early gunning days, with structural features unlike any work recognized as Laing's it was almost certainly not made by him. This bird has no influence on his carving style, but suggested that the first decoys he used were made by others. (Page 22)

A reasonable answer to the question of why Laing made canvasbacks, though he recorded shooting only one, is that he hunted them during the period not covered by the journal. If this explanation is

Laing's house in Stratford as it appeared 60 years after his death.

correct, it follows that he brought all of his canvasback decoys with him when he moved to Connecticut.

Laing was 52 years old when he settled in Stratford, and had been hunting for well over half of his life. By this time he probably had all the decoys he felt he needed. Not only canvasbacks, but also the rest of his decoys, must have been brought to Stratford at the time of his move. This would account for the lack of mention of decoy making in his journal. His principal place of residence had been New York City, and it seems likely that this is where he made most of his decoys.

Several brant by Laing turned up in Virginia. One, with a turned-back head, is shown in Mackey's book and incorrectly attributed to Holmes. Another, with a tucked head, is shown on page 31. The existence of these brant and other Virginia birds, including a sleeping swan, by Laing, indicate that he spent a lot of time hunting in the South before the Civil War. If so, being a Northerner, he might have felt uncomfortable there during the War and been inclined to transfer his activity to a more friendly locality. It is conceivable that this was a factor in his decision to settle in Stratford.

The decoys in Laing's possession at the time of his death were mostly of the classic style with rounded body and pointed spade-like tail, with both straight and turned-back heads—the kind that are easily recognized as Laings. But there were a few that were different—made with thinner bodies and bottom boards.

A group of very old Stratford black ducks with low heads, half-inch bottom boards and a "Holmesy" look, that were formerly attributed to Holmes are now assigned to Laing and are recognized as the prototype for Holmes' earliest black ducks.

One of these black ducks was shown to Roswell Bliss, who, in about 1960, said it was made by Laing. For years Bliss' statement was discredited because of the resemblance to other birds by Holmes and because the shape of the breast seemed uncharacteristic of Laing. The breast is narrow like a Holmes, but the back is flatter and has a shallow trough leading from the neck, and the sides come together to a blunt point at the rump, all typical of Laing. The bill is carved in the manner of other Laing birds, with pointed narrow nostrils and without the mandible separation found on all Holmes' bills. The head is attached by a screw from beneath, rather than by nails, and there are fewer nails in the bottom-board than in Holmes' decoys. Laing presumably brought these birds to Stratford along with his other decoys.

Nearly identical birds from Stratford are branded "B. H. Weller." Some of the bills are notched at the base to depict separate mandibles, but it seems likely that a later owner made this alteration to the bills.

The shape of the breast of these birds is especially noteworthy, for it demonstrates that Laing, rather than Holmes, introduced the design. Laing may have made the narrow breasted birds for use in swift water. The form is best adapted to Stratford conditions and would logically be copied there. The Laing bottom-board blacks were probably leakers, and were given by Laing to his young neighbors, Ben Holmes and Bruce Weller, who used them as patterns. Holmes adhered to the bottom-board method of construction because it was easier than the mid-seam method, but he overcame the leaking tendency by filling the joint with white lead and placing the nails very close together.

In addition to the bottom-board blacks, Laing probably gave Holmes other decoys that were in need of repair. Most of the existing classic straight-head Laing black ducks have heads made by Holmes.

Why Laing old squaws are not found is a puzzling question with seemingly only three possible answers: 1) he shot old squaws over decoys of other species (possibly whistlers); 2) he used old squaw decoys made by others; or 3) he disposed of his old squaw decoys, being of bottom-board construction, for the same reason that he gave his bottom-board black ducks to Ben Holmes and Bruce Weller.

An old old squaw with a three-quarter-inch bottom board and many Laing features was in Bliss' possession at his death, branded "BALDWIN" and "BLISS." It has the general body contour and graceful head shape of a Laing, and the typical shallow groove leading from the neck about one-third the length of the back. The head is slightly inletted at the back of the neck and attached by cut nails; the body sections are also joined by cut nails. The bill carving is slightly different from that of other species of recognized Laings. This bird, that might have been made by Laing, or possibly by Weller, is noteworthy because it seems to have been the model for a family of hollow-carved and balsa old squaws made by Wheeler and Bliss. A twin brother old squaw and a whistler of the same style, each branded "BALDWIN," are in the Shelburne Museum collection (Pages 122 and 123).

The evolution of Laing's decoy form seems to have proceeded through several stages. First was the shallow body design with flat bottom board and iron nails, next the thicker bodied bottom-board form, and finally the "classic" deep-bodied mid-seam style, with copper nails holding the two halves together. Heads were attached in several ways: by a wooden peg or dowel supplemented by a few small nails; by a screw leading from the upper body section; and in some cases by nails only. Both sleepers and straight-heads were made at all stages of the development. Heads of broadbills and canvasbacks were attached to an extension of the upper body section that formed part of the neck. In all turn-backs the head rests on an inclined platform, higher in front. This is an essential feature for attribution of Laing turn-backs. It was not often copied.

Laing as an old man. His last photograph.

Other details common to all Laing decoys, that aid or are prerequisites to identification, are shown in the following list:

1. Bodies are carefully shaped and well finished.
2. Shoulder carving, in the form of a shallow groove, extends fairly far down the middle of the back, unlike Holmes' in which the depression is wider, deeper, and shorter.
3. Eyes, if present and original, are naturally and symmetrically placed.
4. The corner of the mouth is incised in a "c" shape and the lower part of the "c" continues under the bill to form a "v"-shaped chin.

Solid black duck with "LAING" brand, from Long Island. Probably used during the first gunning period of his journal (1831-36). Private collection.

5. Carved mandible separation is not shown as in Holmes' decoys, and a well-defined nail is present on top and bottom of most bills.

6. Nostrils are carved with rounded or pointed ends, not squared as in Holmes' birds.

7. A delicately carved line separates the face from the bill. At the top of the bill, where most other makers made a "v"-cut, the line is finely scribed, usually in the form of an inverted Gothic arch. This seems to have been more a painting guide that a sculptural detail, but is useful for identification.

Laing's classic decoys are units of flowing curves showing perfect balance between head, breast, body, rump, and tail. The breast is rounded, and the rounded sides come together to a blunt point under a flat spade-shaped tail. They are made from two pieces of wood of equal thickness, hollowed out and held together by cut or hand-wrought copper nails, set about one and a one-half inches apart and countersunk, with white lead filling. Laing was the first to make turned-backs or sleepers, and nearly as many of his decoys are found as sleepers as with the straight head position. Strangely, none with a slightly turned head is known.

Eyes were scribed and painted for most species, but some black ducks had black glass bead eyes. Most surviving Laing decoys have been repainted, and are depicted as drakes. They are fitted with various kinds of weights; most are replacements. Strips of lead or long lead bars appear to be the original weights found on some. It is doubtful that Laing used the typical Stratford tear-drop weight, though some of his decoys were fitted with them later, especially by Ben Holmes. Anchor lines were attached by an eye-screw or a leather holding strap. Laing branded some, but not all, of his decoys. Later owners used their personal brands, "F. BURRITT" being a common one.

Though Stratford has now been shown to be the adopted, rather than the native, home of the Laing decoys, it was here that they established their reputation for quality. Laing was the originator of an artistic sculptural form modeled from live ducks rather than from other decoys, unlike the practice of so many of his followers, who copied him and one another.

Laing had a strong influence on carvers of the Delaware River region as well as Connecticut. Evidence is provided by a group of decoys that turned up about 1970, and were reported to have come from Philadelphia. They were a Laing broadbill of intermediate body thickness and two pintails, a high-

Bottom of solid Long Island black duck, showing "LAING" brand.

head and a sleeper, made by Laing's first cousin, R. W. Davids. All of these birds are hollow, with three-fourths-inch to one-inch bottom boards and fitted with rectangular weights of sheet lead. Both sleepers are branded "C. W. MORRIS" and the Laing is also branded "R. W. DAVIDS." It has been established that these are brands of Richard Wistar Davids (1825-1863) and Charles Wistar Morris (1824-1893), cousins of about the same age who lived in Philadelphia and hunted together. It is likely that Laing, with his family ties, hunted with the pair. He no doubt gave the broadbill to Davids.

When Davids died in 1863 (the same year that Laing moved to Stratford), he probably left his entire gunning rig to Morris. A sleeping redhead, of the same form as the sleeping pintail, found in Elkton, Maryland, and branded "R. W. DAVIDS," was originally from the same rig. A reasonable guess at a date for the Davids birds is 1845-50, and for the Laing probably earlier.

The importance attached to these decoys is the similarity between them and the birds by John Blair and other Delaware River carvers who followed Laing and Davids, and who seem to have imitated them. Laing was apparently the first to make hollow-carved decoys and sleepers. The sleeper form, that Davids copied from Laing, never gained much popularity among his Philadelphia neighbors, but the hollow body and its general contour were adopted by contemporary and later carvers of the area.

Laing was a man of medium size. As a youth he wore mutton-chop whiskers and, when older, a full beard. He was not gregarious. He never married and seems to have been at odds with his family. He was dropped as a member of his father's business operation and was not included in his father's will. Most of his hunting was done alone, but he did mention one man with whom he hunted, "Alibi" Edwards.

During the last fifteen years of his life, Laing did no hunting and his health seemed to be failing. After several months of severe headache and depression, on October 18, 1886, he shot himself with his double-barreled fowling piece. The last entry in his journal, written five years earlier, reads "The martins left today."

At his death, Laing left one hundred eleven decoys, which he specified were to be sold for $45 (about 40 cents each). Roughly half of them were branded. They went first to the Beers family, who sold some to Francis Burritt and Cappy Wicks. Later a good many were acquired by Shang Wheeler, who repaired and

Early Laing black duck with narrow breast and bottom board. The Ben Holmes prototype. Private collection.

Early Laing bottom-board black duck branded "B.H.WELLER". Swanson Collection.

Very old Stratford Stratford black duck with Laing features. Possibly an early Laing or Weller. Private collection.

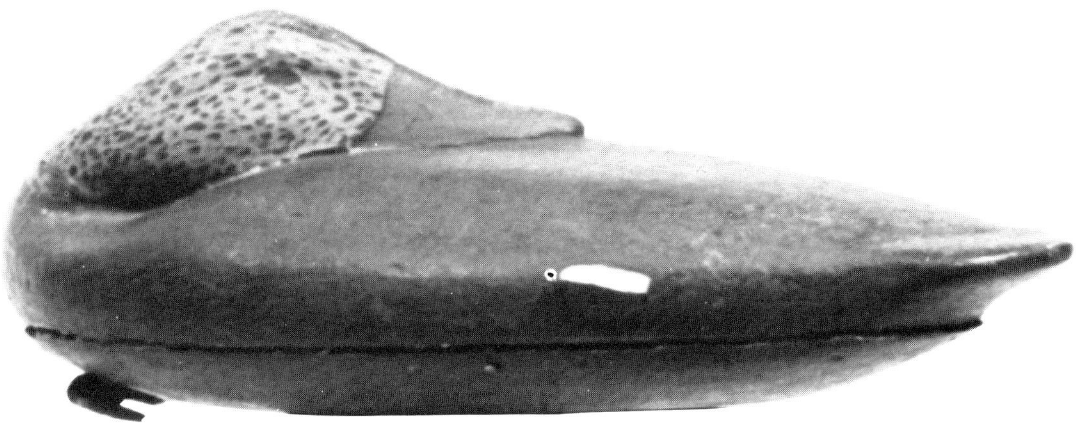

Laing sleeper. Originally a canvasback. Repainted as a black duck. Wm. Doyle Galleries.

repainted them and used them for gunning. In 1934 some of these, along with various other used decoys, 150 in all, were sold to Tom Marshall for $1.50 apiece. Marshall used the lot for gunning until the Laings became quite valuable and then, about 1970, sold them to David Rockefeller.

Whether or not Laing made shorebird decoys is problematical. There is no convincing evidence that he did. In any case he shot only a few shorebirds, mostly yellowlegs, and it is likely that he came upon them more by accident than by design.

Laing bottom-board canvasback. Private collection.

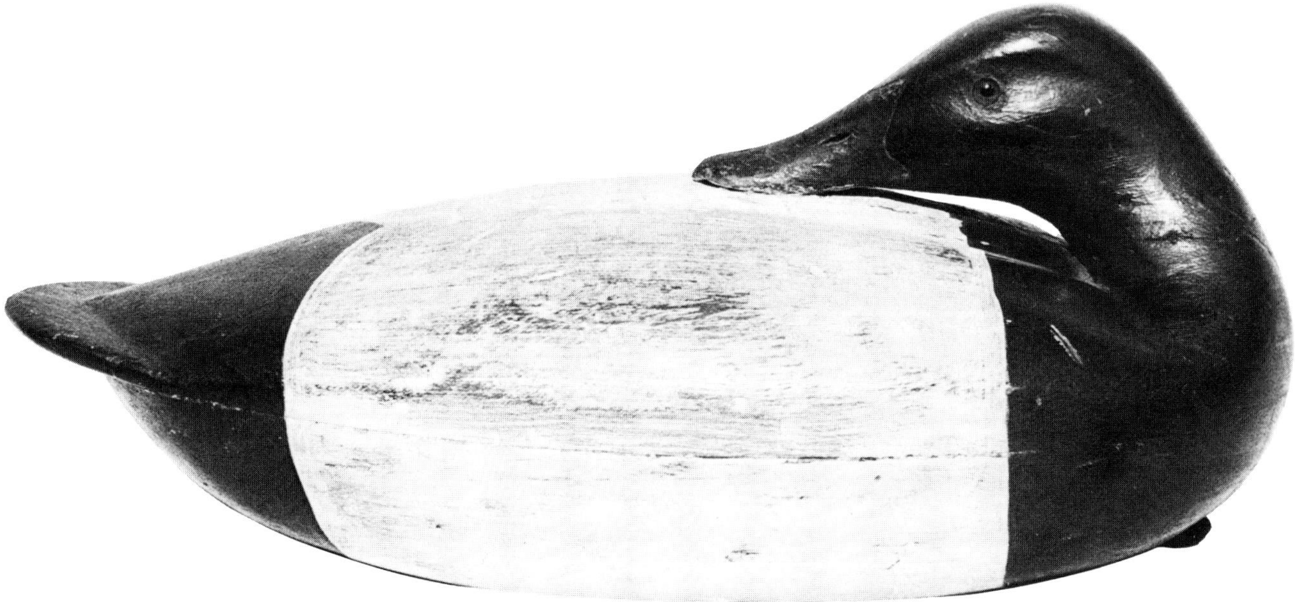

Classic Laing canvasback. Private collection.

Laing canvasback painted as a black duck. Note head attached to a high neck extension from the body. Shelburne Museum.

Laing turned-head canvasback painted by Wheeler as a black duck. Shelburne Museum.

Classic Laing straight-head black duck. Head replaced by Holmes. Shelburne Museum.

Bottom of the preceding Laing black duck.

Classic Laing broadbill sleeper. Private collection.

Another classic Laing broadbill sleeper. Head turned in opposite direction. Private collection.

Laing drake goldeneye with "BALDWIN" brand over "LAING". Swanson collection.

Another classic Laing goldeneye. Shelburne Museum.

Classic Laing black duck sleeper. Collection of Michael and Julie Hall.

Laing scoter converted to a black. Private collection.

Laing black duck. Early shallow decoy with bottom-board. Private collection.

Very early Laing brant (perhaps 1835). Collection of Ron Swanson.

Dowell fastening head to body of Laing brant, showing "LAING" carving. Private collection.

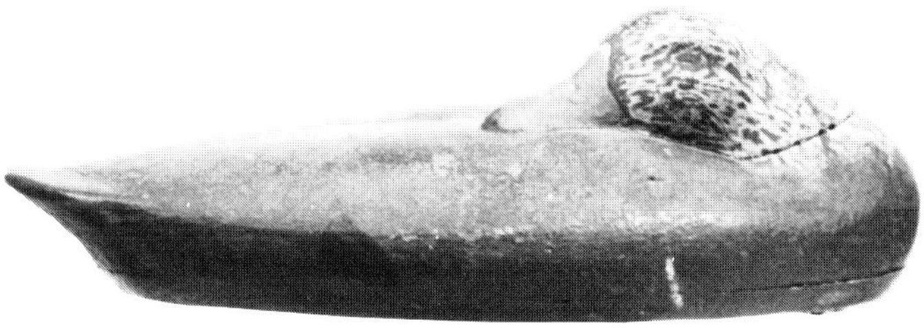

Another Laing bottom-board black duck. Private collection.

Laing pintail painted by Shang Wheeler for Tom Marshall. Private collection.

Pintails by R. W. Davids—original paint, c. 1845-50. Note the strong Laing influence on style. Private collection.

Broadbill from the Laing-Davids group after restoration. Branded "R. W. DAVIDS" and "C. W. MORRIS", the "W" in each case for Wistar, a family name. Collection of Clune Walsh.

Redhead sleeper by R. W. Davids, c. 1845-50. Very similar to Laing, but head attachment different. Collection of Michael and Julie Hall.

Laing black, foreground, with unidentified old black duck, possibly by Weller.

Benjamin Holmes.

BENJAMIN HOLMES (1843-1912)

Benjamin Holmes, one of seven children of William and Abigail Coley Holmes, was born and lived his entire life in Stratford. His father drove a stagecoach between New Haven and Stamford. When Benjamin was 19 years old, he apprenticed himself to S. R. Bruce, a Stratford carpenter, and after fifteen years, went into business for himself.

Ben Holmes was responsible for the construction of many important buildings in the area, but is known best for his narrow-stern skiffs and especially for his decoys. The skiffs, in 14- and 18-foot lengths, with each side constructed of a single 18-inch plank, were popular with duck hunters. Unlike Laing, Wheeler, and others who made decoys for their own use, Holmes was not a duck hunter, and made decoys strictly for sale.

After Laing set the style and standard of excellence for Stratford decoys, the most successful of his followers was Ben Holmes, who was thirty-two years his junior. Holmes' early work nearly duplicated Laing's, but later he incorporated his own modifications and produced beautiful and serviceable birds that gained him a reputation rivaling that of Laing. According to the story so often repeated, Holmes won a prize at the 1876 Philadelphia Centennial Exposition for a dozen broadbill decoys he entered. Many of these so-called "Centennial" decoys, which sold for $30 a dozen, were made and shipped to buyers all over the United States.

For the local market Holmes made broadbills, black ducks, and whistlers. Several of his mergansers have been found in Stratford, and a few brant have been attributed to him. For the southern gunning areas he made also, on special order, canvasbacks and redheads. He increased the body thickness as his carving progressed. Broadbills became slightly deeper, and for black ducks and whistlers there was a distinct change from early low-backed to later high-backed forms.

Holmes' method of construction was to saw out the body, using patterns, so that the final individuals from a given production run were identical. He then shaped the bodies, and from this point followed two different courses. For his early Laing copies, he sliced off a half-inch section from the bottom, using a band saw. He then hollowed the main upper section and replaced the bottom. Evidence for this can be seen in the wood grain that goes continuously through the body and bottom board. Following his second, and more to be expected, course, he made the main body and bottom sections separately. He then sealed the bottom board, usually one-half inch thick, but occasionally slightly thinner or thicker, with white lead and nailed it to the body. The head was commonly attached to the body by nailing, using five nails, but in some species the head was held on by a screw from beneath, supplemented by a few nails from the top.

In addition to the characteristic bottom-board, Holmes decoys have several other distinguishing features. The narrow breast, though copied from Laing, is typical of Holmes and not found in the classic Laings. The breasts are pointed in all species, most prominently in canvasbacks and redheads, and least so in whistlers. The sides of Holmes decoys, while gracefully curved, join the flat bottom more abruptly than in the case of Laing. The rise from the neck to the high point of the back is steeper in Holmes ducks, and the rumps are more rounded than Laing's. Laing's duck decoys were made uniformly with pointed tails. Holmes followed this style with his black ducks and whistlers, but made all other species with flat-ended or rounded tails.

The original eyes of most broadbills and whistlers were painted, but other species are commonly found with glass eyes. Holmes weights are narrow tear-drop in shape with one screw hole and a pointed end, which was often held in place by a tack or small staple. X-ray photographs of Holmes birds show a beautiful pattern of parallel closely spaced nails,

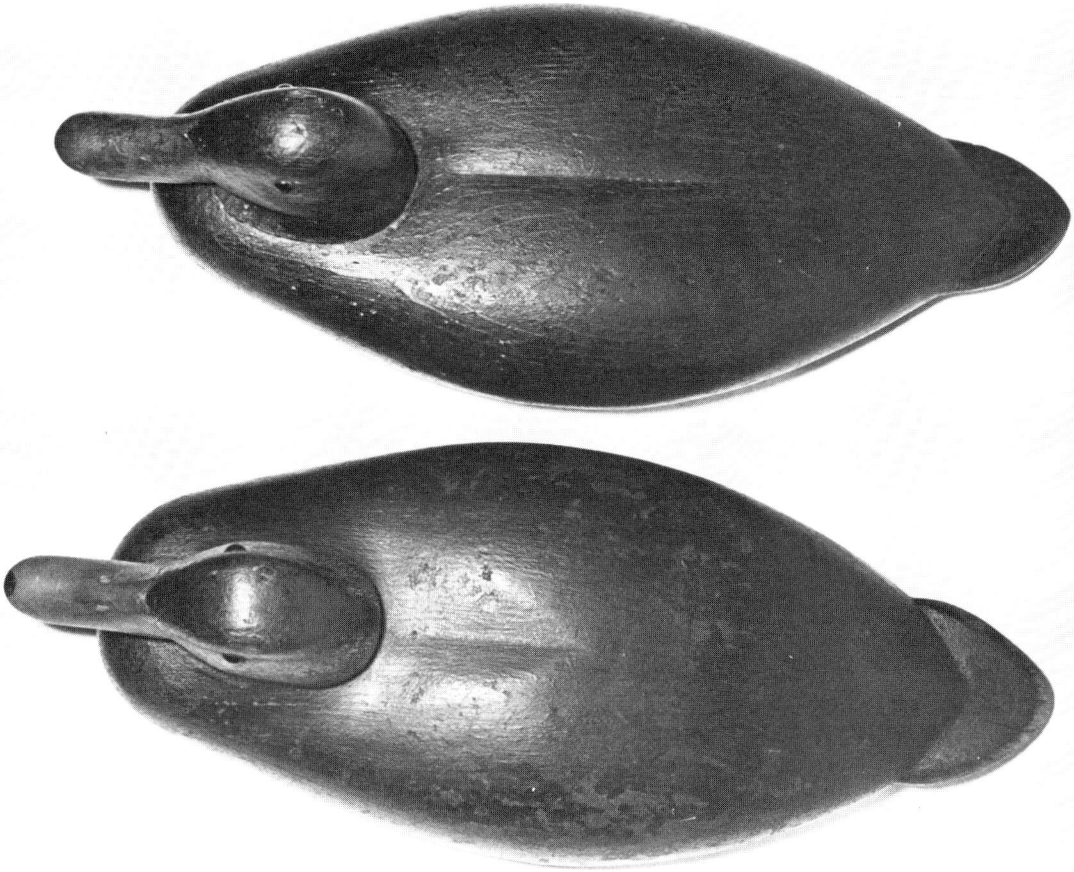

Holmes and Laing black ducks.

Holmes and Laing black ducks.

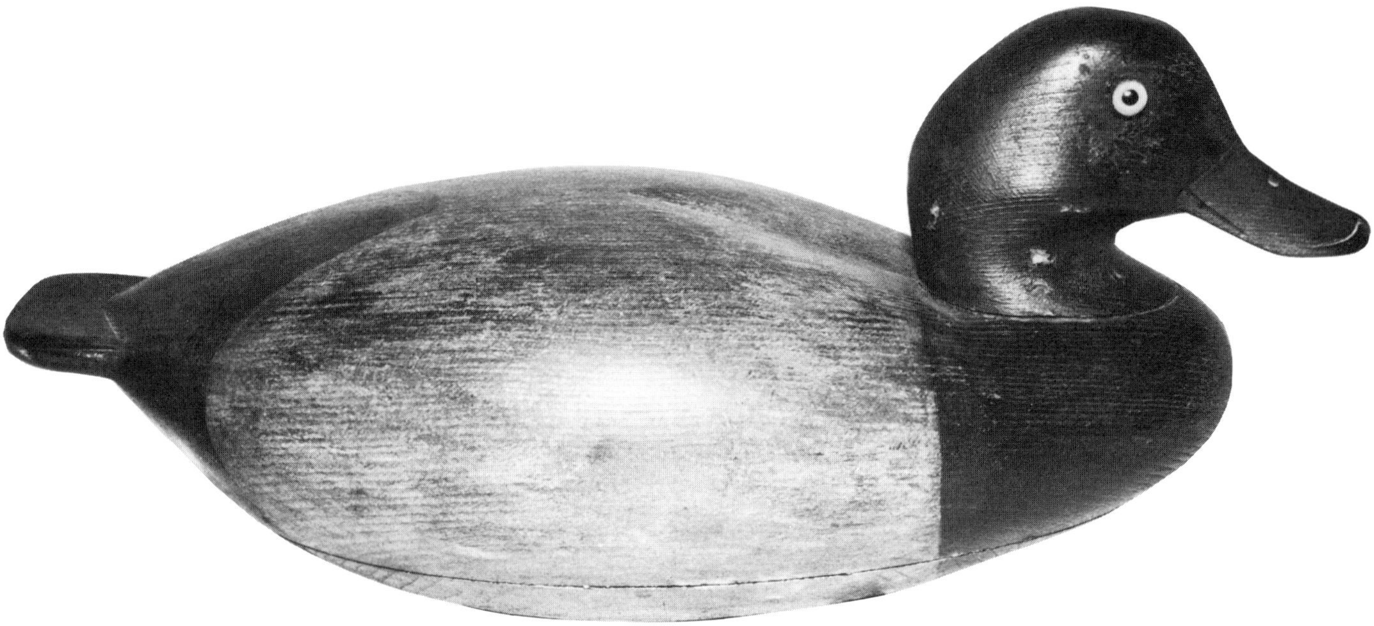

Holmes low-backed broadbill. Probably his earlier style. Shelburne Museum collection.

varying in number from 22 for his earlier birds up to 35 for his later black ducks. He used forged or cut nails initially but switched to wire finishing nails later, probably before 1900.

The excellence of Holmes' craftsmanship is seen in the heads that are gracefully rounded without abrupt angles. A narrow cut to show mandible separation ends at the base of the bill in a deep indentation that gives the duck a "smiling" appearance. The Laing characteristic of a "v" chin or raised angular extension of the neck is seen where it joins the underside of the bill in most species. The bill is usually tipped with a carved nail. Nostrils are prominent and have squared ends. A small "B. HOLMES" is stamped or branded into the wood on some decoys. On others it is lacking, either because it was not applied or, being lightly indented, it may have become obliterated in use.

Laing did not design his decoys for use in Stratford—they were made elsewhere—but Holmes adapted his birds specifically to the local conditions. Generally, Holmes breasts slant from the top inward to ride better through choppy water. Heads always look directly foreward, never in even a slightly turned direction. Holmes did not make sleepers, possibly because Laing gave him none to be used as patterns or because their demand by local customers was not sufficient to justify the greater difficulty of construction.

It is not known whether Holmes ever made mid-seam birds or how much he might have departed from his conventional style. Very old decoys with Holmes-like features are found, some with mid-seams. They may represent work of an early experimental period, before he settled on the final patterns for large-scale production.

No Laing prototype for Holmes broadbills has been identified, and heretofore no one has suggested that Holmes copied his broadbill design from Laing, but in view of Laing's versatility and the apparent Laing-Holmes relationship, the possibility exists. The carving details of some unidentified Stratford broadbills suggest that Laing might have made some of them and that Weller and Holmes made others. Whatever its derivation, the Holmes broadbill is universally recognized as the archetype of the Stratford School. Culver, Lattin, Willard Baldwin, Bliss, and others used it as a model. It has been the popular style most imitated in and around Stratford for over a hundred years.

Another low-backed Holmes broadbill. Private collection.

Bottom view of Holmes broadbill drake showing "B. HOLMES" stamp, weight, and placement of nails. Private collection.

Holmes scaup drake. The "Centenniel" model of 1876. Private collection.

Holmes broadbill drake, later model. Private collection.

Holmes hen broadbill. Private collection.

Black duck by Ben Holmes. Early low-backed Laing style. Shelburne Museum collection.

Low-backed Holmes black duck. Private collection.

High-backed, later style Holmes black duck. Shelburne Museum collection.

High-backed Holmes black duck. Private collection.

Holmes black duck; high-backed form. Shelburne Museum.

Brant attributed to Ben Holmes. Private collection.

Holmes whistlers of different design. Both have original heads. The female (with broken bill) was repainted by Wheeler. Private collection.

Holmes hen whistler, low-backed form. Reheaded and painted by Wheeler. Shelburne Museum.

Early Holmes whistler. Private collection.

Holmes whistler. Early wide-breasted style. This bird was repainted by Wheeler. Ron Swanson collection.

This blocky-headed goldeneye, though unlike Holmes' other work, has been generally attributed to Holmes. Shelburne Museum.

Holmes last style whistler, with a very high back. Private collection.

Holmes redhead. Used in a Currituck Sound, North Carolina, gunning club. Branded "WRP" and "FBA". Private collection.

Holmes canvasback used in a Currituck Sound gunning club. From the same rig as the redhead. Private collection.

Bottom view of Holmes canvasback showing brands of two successive owners. Private collection.

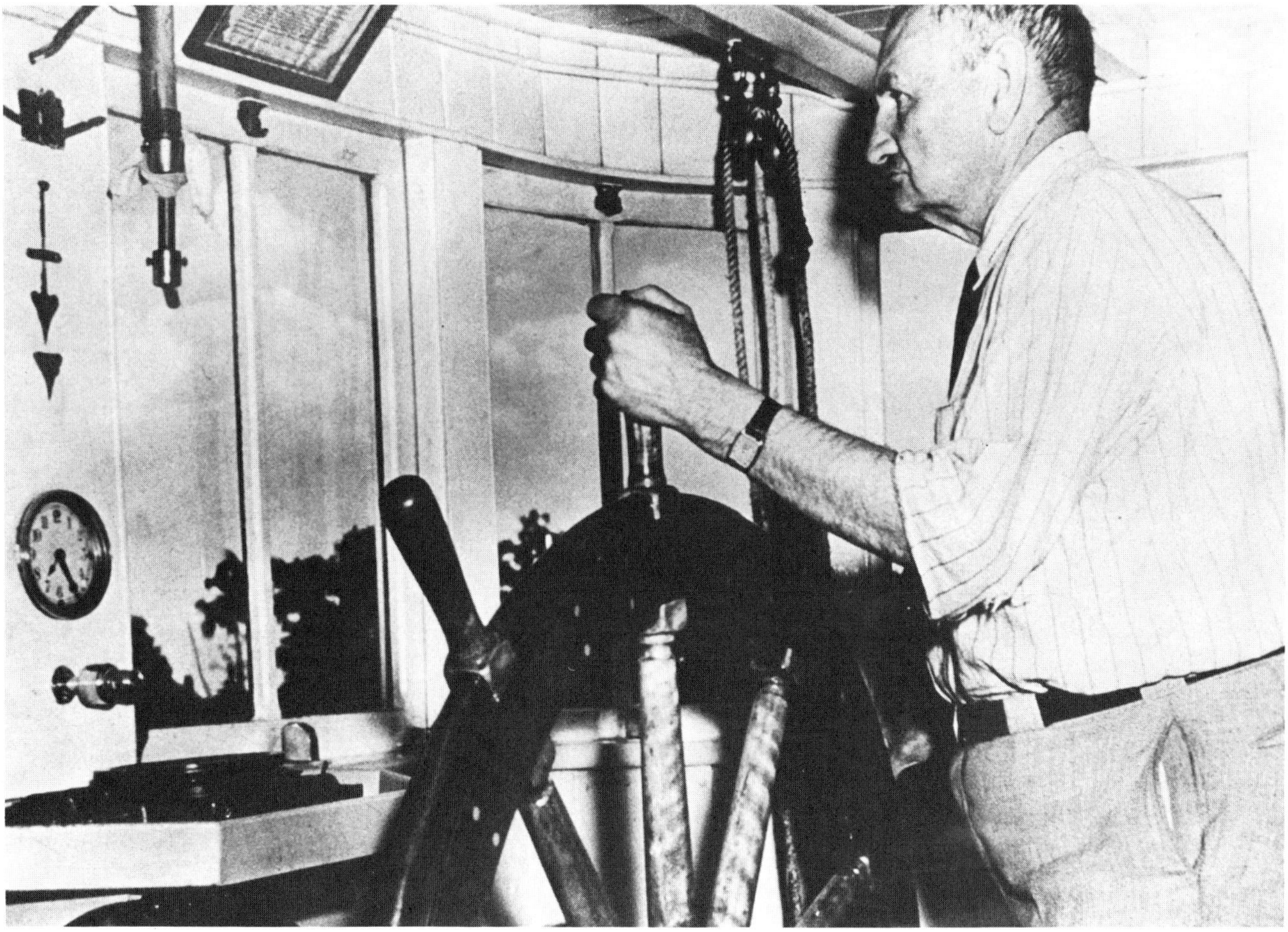

Shang Wheeler at the helm of his pleasure boat.
Courtesy of Mrs. Thomas C. Marshall.

CHARLES EDWARD WHEELER (1872-1949)

Charles Edward Wheeler was known to everyone as "Shang". He was Connecticut's most famous decoy maker and had great influence in stimulating nationwide interest in decoy carving and collecting. He was also an outstanding citizen—an artist, conservationist, civic leader, and politician who was always willing to help those in financial need or seeking advice on the subject in which he was the ultimate authority, the making of decoys.

Shang Wheeler was a large man who got his nickname because of his stature, his friends comparing him to a giant of the period named Chang who was with P.T. Barnum's circus. His highest formal education was at the Weston Military School. He ran away from home and for a while hand-lined for cod on a commercial fishing boat off the Grand Banks. For five years he acted as a guide in the Florida swamps. After tow-boating in New York and natural oystering in the Housatonic River, he finally settled down to a permanent job with the Stratford Oyster Company, where he stayed as manager through several changes of ownership until the time of his death.

Wheeler's political career included two terms in the Connecticut State Legislature, one term in the State Senate, six years on the Pollution Committee and six years as a Commissioner of Fisheries and Game. He was active in many sporting, political, business, and civic groups. As a skilled and creative artist, he used his talent in painting pictures of waterfowl, designing his own Christmas cards, and in the interest of conservation, through a series of cartoons published in the Bridgeport Sunday Post.

He started as a market gunner and his first working stools were simple wide-bodied flat blocks carved from solid pine, with either raised or tucked-down heads. Another form, used over a period of years, had a flat natural cork body with a simply carved dowelled head and a wooden keel with a section of flattened lead tubing nailed on for ballast. This style was dressed up much later for working class show competition, but with bodies of composite cork, delicately carved heads, and fancy paint.

Wheeler liked to hunt and many of his decoys were made solely for that purpose, but he also enjoyed drawing, painting, and carving. It was the combination of his sporting and artistic interests that led him to produce his outstanding carvings of waterfowl, other birds, and fish. As an artist he was not content with endlessly duplicating a pattern. Though the influence of Laing can be seen in much of his work, he continued to innovate and developed a wide spectrum of decoy designs. At one end are the simple, crudely finished flat cork workers, and at the other end are the gracefully carved and meticulously painted show class birds that dominated the competition of all the national shows for so many years. In between are a great variety of working decoys of high quality, constructed with care and artistry but with less attention to perfection of paint. Among them are regular size and slightly oversize black ducks of hollow pine and black ducks and canvasbacks of cork composite. Geese and most of the other species, including scaup, mallard, golden-eye, widgeon, pintail, and scoter, were made of hollow pine, but there exist a few solid examples as well as some of balsa. Except in his earliest birds, Wheeler seemed to have an aversion to the directly forward head position. Most of the heads face slightly to one side or the other. He also made turned-heads or sleepers.

He worked closely with Bliss, who made some of the birds that have been credited to Wheeler. He helped Bliss with the painting of at least one order of decoys made for sale in South Carolina, but accepted no pay for this. Most of the decoys made by him that left his possession went as gifts, but he did sell a few, and on occasion made and sold a dozen or so on special order.

When making black duck decoys in quantity for his own use or sale he evolved a speedy production line method of painting the feathers instead of the free-hand method used for his show birds. A paper pattern was prepared with holes indicating the shape and position of each feather. It was wrapped around the bird and dusted with talcum powder, leaving a feather pattern that could be quickly followed with an artist's brush. During his period of competitive carving (1923-1948) no one came close to equalling his success until near the end when Louis Rathmell, following Wheeler's style, finally won out over the old master in a few categories.

Wheeler used many old decoys of other makers, which he accumulated around Stratford and Milford. At one time he owned most of the existing Laings, many by Holmes, Cassius Smith, the Smith brothers, and others. He maintained them in working condition by repainting and repair. A majority of the existing decoys by the old well-known Stratford makers show his handiwork.

At his death he left a collection of about 75 show-class ducks, along with other carvings including a sandhill crane, a striped bass, an Atlantic salmon, and ten working scoters. Tom Marshall was asked by the attorney for the estate to dispose of these items but to keep together the show decoys, which were to be sold for a total of $1,000. The attorney suggested that the remaining decoys and carvings be kept by Marshall as his fee. The show birds were first bought by C. K. Davis of Remington Arms, who soon decided he really did not want them. Through a campaign for contributions, Marshall acquired them and they were donated to the Audubon Birdcraft Museum in Fairfield, where they remained until 1983 when they were sold to a private collector.

Shang Wheeler at the Grand Central Palace Decoy Show, c. 1948.

Wheelers exhibition at the 1948 National Decoy Makers Show.

ONAL DECOY MAKERS
CONTEST
AND EXHIBITION
Sponsored by R. J. SCHAEFER
sident The F. & M. Schaefer Brewing Co.
In Coo ration with
SHELDON FAIRBANKS
ident Campbell- airbanks Expositions, Inc.
I may not be the finest decoy
in the Show · But -
Schaefer
is the Finest Beer I Ever Tasted
Special Exhibit by

The author with one of Shang Wheeler's "sneak" boats. Now the property of Shelburne Museum.

Female scaup. An example of the quickly-made gunning birds made and used by Wheeler.

Wheeler. Simply constructed cork-bodied scoter with a well-carved head. Private collection.

Wheeler scaup drake with a simple flat cork body but a more carefully carved head. Swanson collection.

Black duck by Wheeler in the Laing style. Shelburne Museum.

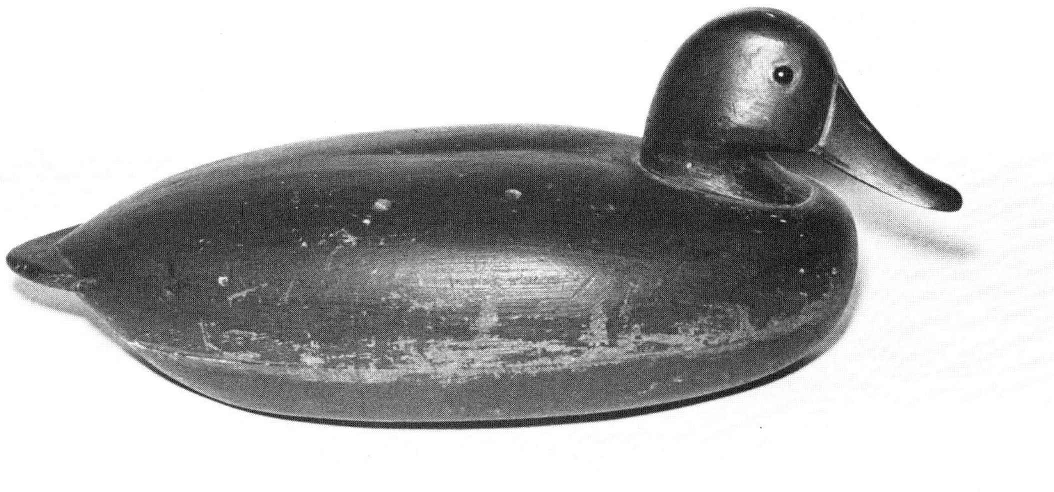

Early Wheeler black duck, lacking the fine painting of his later birds. (End of bill has been replaced.) Private collection.

One of a group of decoys taken from Connecticut to Cleveland in 1925. The heads and weights are definitely Wheeler's. Though the bottom edges are a little less rounded than in his later work, these birds are attributed to Wheeler. Private collection.

Wheeler old squaw, c. 1890s. Ron Swanson collection.

Wheeler old squaw. This bird had been repainted as a whistler, the repaint removed, and the original paint restored and retouched. Bottom-board construction. Bourne auction.

Old squaw attributed to Wheeler. Mid-seam construction. Private collection.

Wheeler old squaw, exhibition grade drake. Private collection.

Wheeler old squaw, exhibition grade duck. Private collection.

Wheeler competition grade scaup. Private collection.

Wheeler working balsa white-winged scoter. Private collection.

Wheeler working pintail of unusual solid construction. Swanson collection.

Wheeler working canvasback. Cork body. Private collection.

Working canvasback hen by Wheeler, c. 1932. From Wolcott rig. Swanson collection.

Wheeler balsa brant. Private collection.

Wheeler brant of hollow wood construction. Private collection.

Wheeler black duck of exhibition quality. Private collection.

Cork-bodied Wheeler goose. Found in Lake Erie area. Swanson collection.

Finely carved and finished Wheeler goose. Private collection.

Wheeler. Exhibition grade green-winged teal. Private collection.

Francis Burritt.

FRANCIS BURRITT

Francis Burritt deserves the notice of collectors because so many fine Laing and Holmes decoys have been traced back to him through his brands "F. BURRITT" and "F. B." He was born in New York City in 1850 and moved to South Norwalk, Connecticut, where he became a designer and racer of sailing yachts. He was a founder of the Indian Harbor Yacht Club in Greenwich and Commodore of the Cedar Point Yacht Club. A book on the history of yachting published in 1894 stated that he had (up to that time) owned twenty-three yachts and that "few yachtsmen have done more to advance yachting and racing on Long Island Sound than Commodore Francis Burritt." Besides avid pursuit of yachting, he seems also to have had a great interest in—and plenty of time for—duck hunting, much of it around Stratford. Though often mentioned as a gunning companion of Laing, this is highly improbable. Laing was a loner and stopped gunning when Burritt was only twenty years old. Burritt died in 1928 at the age of 78.

CAPPY WICKS

The name "Cappy" Wicks is well known among Stratford hunters. Charles Delancey Wicks, Sr. was born in Seaford, Long Island in 1860 and as a young man moved to Stratford, where he established an oyster and lobster business. He was owner and captain of several working boats, the best known being the "Gertrude S. Terry". He was a market hunter and the leading guide for sportsmen of the Housatonic area for many years. The *Bridgeport Sunday Post* of November 10, 1912 carried a half-page spread on duck hunting which featured him. The article mentioned as well-known Stratford hunters of the time, Kenneth Peck, William V. Austin, "Shang" Wheeler, Allen MacGregor, Lew Polly, Walter Wheeler, Allan Beardsley, Anson Dart, and E. P. Allen, as well as the following out-of-towners who hunted with Wicks: Samuel Senior, Earnest G. Southey, Nat Wheeler, Leon Beardsley, Dr. Robert Lynch, Allan W. Paige, Harry Gates, Stanley Kellogg, Dr. J. Henry Callahan, and John T. Hubbard.

Cappy Wicks used more important decoys by Laing, Holmes, and other gifted makers than any other area resident. They were passed down to his son Charles D. Wicks, Jr. (also called Cappy), Shang Wheeler, Joel Barber and later to Ken Peck, Tom Marshall, Bill Mackey and others. It is not known with certainty whether he made any of the great variety of birds he used.

The younger Cappy (1889-1952) was also a duck hunter, as well as a full-time employee of Remington Arms. In addition to the decoys he acquired from his father, he used some made by Bliss. Many of these were embellished by Cappy's own paintings, according to his daughter who watched him spend hours meticulously attending to this task.

BRUCE H. WELLER (1848-1925)

Bruce Weller of Stratford hunted with narrow-breasted bottom-board Laing decoys that he branded "B. H. WELLER." He was a pattern maker and was reported to have made decoys, but none have been unequivocally attributed to him. Black ducks that resemble the narrow-breasted Laings, but of lesser quality and with heavier bodies, have been found in Stratford. It is possible that Weller made these as well as some of the unidentified scaup that have Laing features.

ROSWELL EDWARD BLISS (1887-1967)

Stratford's most prolific producer of decoys and the only one except Ben Holmes who can be considered a true professional was Roswell Bliss. "Roz" or "Blissy", as he was known to his friends, was the last of a line of several generations of New England artisans and builders. He was a pattern maker by

Roswell E. Bliss.

trade, working part of the time in industry, but for many years he conducted his own business at R. E. Bliss Manufacturing Company, in a shop next to his house.

Roswell Bliss was born in Stratford in 1887 and lived there his entire life. He began duck hunting in the marshes of the Housatonic River as a boy of twelve. At age 14 he decided he wanted a set of decoys so he approached Ben Holmes, whom he knew personally, with the intent of buying them. Finding the price higher than he could afford, he decided to make his own. Thus in 1901 he started making decoys, the first group being hollow-carved black ducks.

By 1910 Bliss had settled on a distinctive pear-shaped, flat-bottomed design that makes his decoys easily recognizable. They are strictly "Stratford" in style but less graceful and with more abrupt angles and heavier bills than decoys of Laing or Holmes. Bliss birds are perfectly symmetrical and most have a clearly scribed center line that can be seen on close inspection. Though the patterns were changed from time to time, all individuals from a given manufacturing run are identical in shape, to very close tolerances. There is no deviation in head direction from straight ahead, except for a small number of sleepers made in his later years. The common construction form is a hollow pine body with a three-quarter inch bottom board, but some of the bodies had the seam higher up, and a few on special order were of solid pine. For a time he also used balsa but the number of balsa decoys produced was small. Bliss experimented with heads of cast aluminum but soon abandoned the idea.

Bliss, at an early age, must have acquired the hunting rig of Arthur Baldwin. Many birds bear both brands, and a good many by Baldwin and miscellaneous other makers were repaired, reheaded, and repainted by Bliss. The typical wide-bodied Baldwin scaup have small unattractive bills. Bliss replaced the heads on some of these with stout-billed better looking ones, thereby converting them to handsome decoys.

By 1930 Shang Wheeler had become a good friend. He often visited the shop and sometimes picked up a roughed-out head and carved it as they talked. Occasionally Bliss and Wheeler shared work on decoy orders for friends of the latter in South Carolina. Roswell carved and Shang painted. By 1937 Bliss had become a noted maker of hand-carved hunting decoys. Wheeler interested him in feather painting and instructed him on techniques. After painstaking practice, he became quite skillful.

In 1940 he entered some decoys in the National Decoy Contest in New York City and won many ribbons. He continued to exhibit yearly until the show was discontinued for lack of sponsors. He gradually developed a larger line of show birds featuring full feathering. The Shelburne Museum requested a Canada goose for its collection in 1966.

In the 1950s, upon the urging of his wife Gertrude, Bliss began to carve and paint miniature ducks for table decorations. These became popular collectors' items. In addition he made shore birds, such as yellowlegs, black-breasted plover and curlew, and various song birds.

His earlier work was limited to black ducks, broadbills, mallards and old squaws, but later he added whistlers, three species of scoters, widgeon, pintails, buffleheads, canvasbacks, redheads, teal and wood ducks, as well as brant and Canada geese. His total output of decoys was over 2000.

Bliss continued hunting but with decreasing frequency to the age of 70. Two of his favorite partners were Ken Peck and E. B. Crocker. He worked daily in his shop until hospitalized with a stroke in 1967. He died three days later at age 80 years and 7 months.

Bliss early scaup with bill edges curved inward. Private collection.

R. E. Bliss early broadbill. Private collection.

Bliss scaup duck of later style. Private collection.

Bliss scaup drake of later style. Private collection.

Bliss black duck c. 1910. Private collection.

R. E. Bliss black duck; from the rig made in 1947 for "Cappy" Wicks. Private collection.

Bliss mallard drake, c. 1945. Private collection.

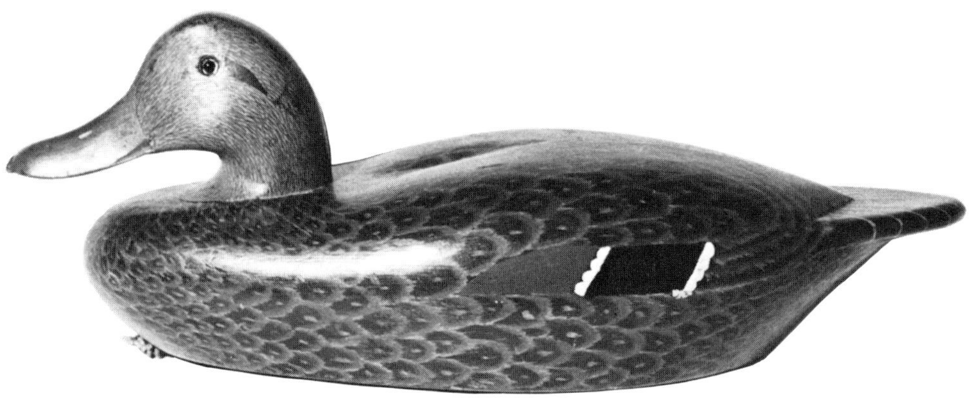

Bliss hen mallard, 1950. Private collection.

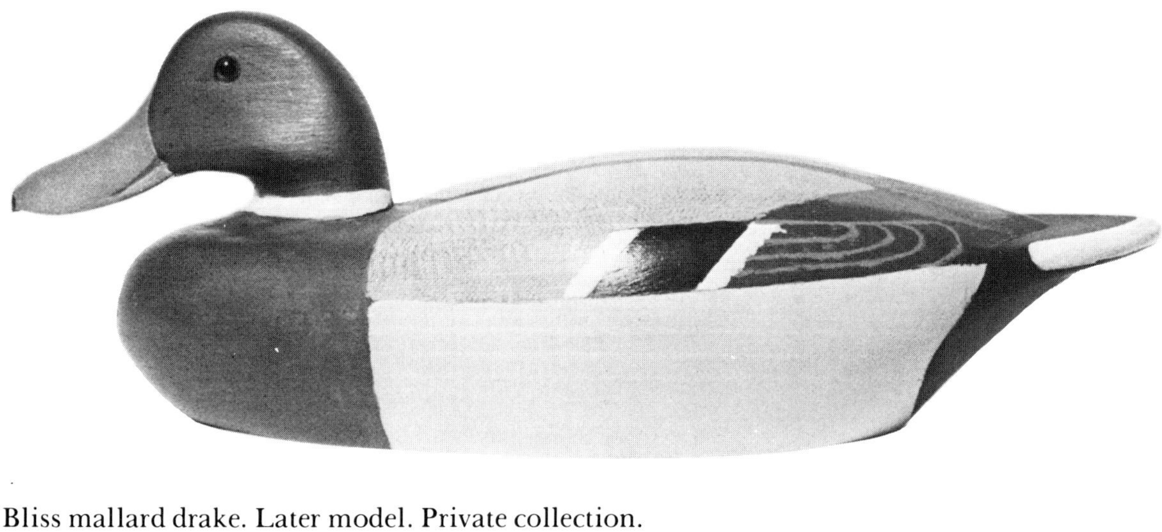

Bliss mallard drake. Later model. Private collection.

Goldeneye duck by Bliss. c. 1945. Private collection.

Balsa old squaw by Wheeler or possibly Bliss. Shelburne Museum.

Bliss goldeneye, 1954. Private collection.

Bliss old squaw, repainted as scaup. Private collection.

Bliss old squaws. Examples of his later work.

Bliss brant. Private collection.

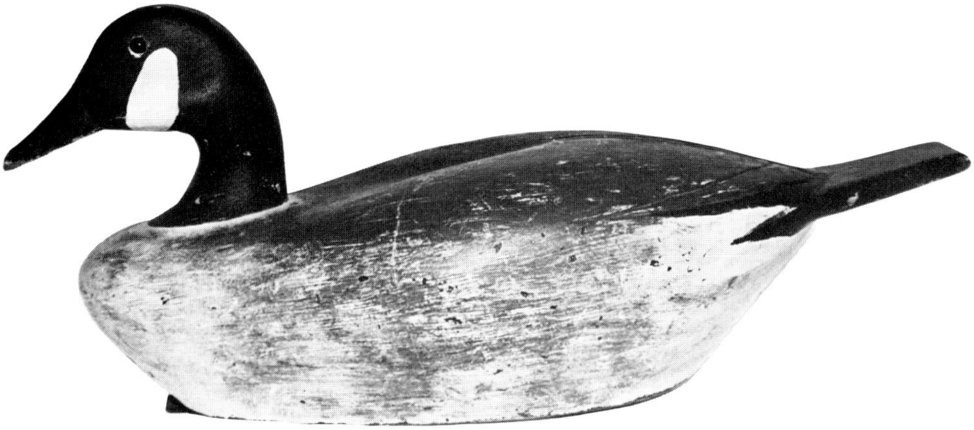

Bliss goose used by Tom Marshall. Private collection.

White-winged scoter by Bliss, c. 1955. Private collection.

Pair of canvasbacks by Bliss. Private collection.

Pair of buffleheads by Bliss. Private collection.

Extremes in size of Bliss ducks. Green-wing teal and oversized black duck. Private collection.

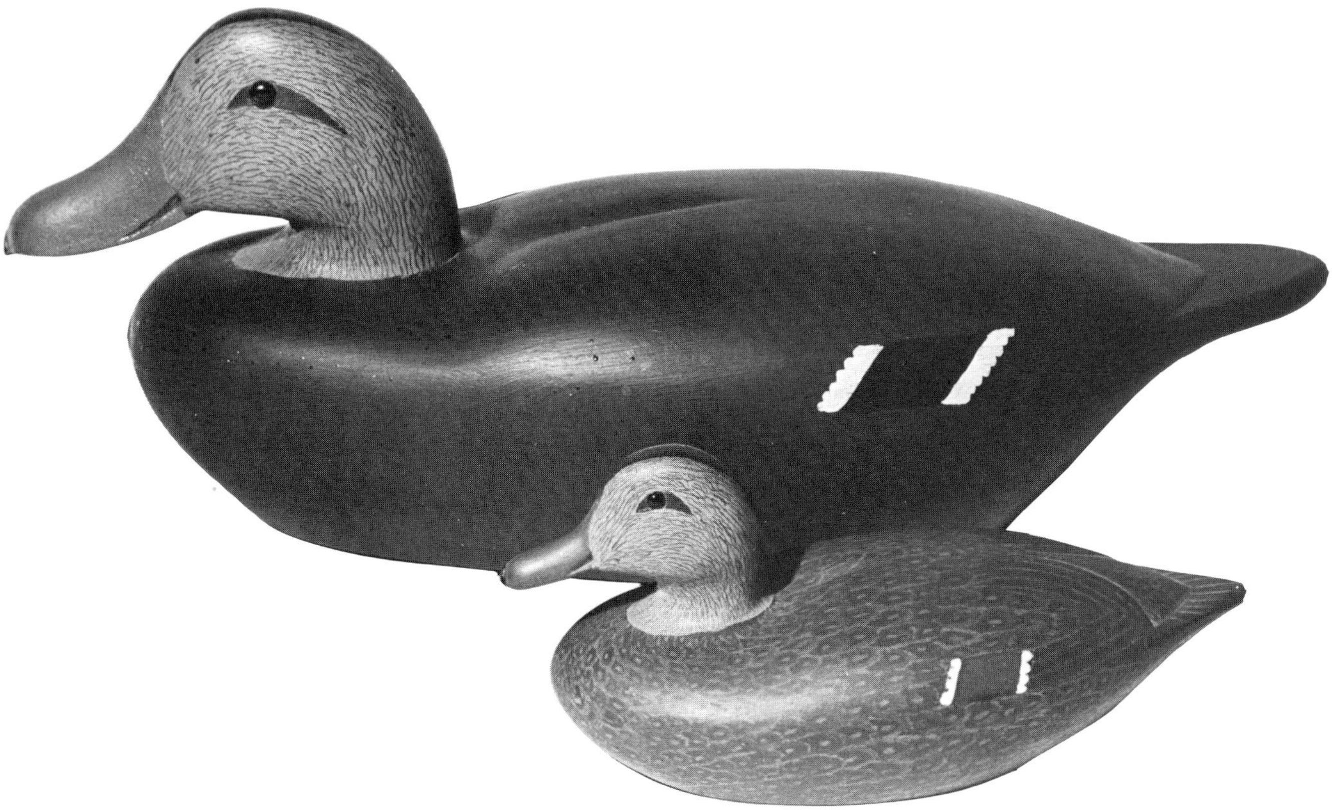

Classic Laing scaup. Private collection.

Laing classic straight-head scaup. Private collection.

Laing surf scoter. Shelburne Museum Collection.

Laing canvasback, painted by Wheeler as a black duck. Shelburne Museum Collection.

Ben Holmes black ducks, showing different head styles. Private collection.

Holmes drake goldeneye—Head replaced by Wheeler. Shelburne Museum.

Holmes merganser. Shelburne Museum Collection.

Wheeler black duck. The body is a single piece of natural cork with an attached keel. Private collection.

Balsa old squaw by Wheeler or Bliss. Shelburne Museum.

Shang Wheeler old squaw. Courtesy of Shelburne Museum.

Wheeler drake canvasback, hollow wood construction. Shelburne Museum.

Wheeler goose of hollow pine, original paint. Private collection.

Mallard drake by Wildfowler Decoys, Old Saybrook. Private collection.

Wildfowler canvasback drake. Private collection.

Green-winged teal owned by Charles R. Disbrow and given to Dr. Nathan Friedman. Private collection.

Mulliken exhibition black duck. Shelburne Museum.

Pintail drake by Harry Ross of Old Saybrook. Private collection.

Joel Barber mallard. Shelburne Museum.

Wheeler gull. Private collection.

Hollow-carved hen wood duck by Shang Wheeler. Private collection.

Hollow-carved drake wood duck by Shang Wheeler. Private collection.

Shang Wheeler wood duck. An example of his most elaborate decorative carving. Bourne Auction House.

Shang Wheeler hen wood duck. Mate to previous bird. Bourne Auction House.

Wood duck by Willard Baldwin, painted by Harold Morse. Private collection.

Bliss pintail drake. Private collection.

Bliss hen pintail. Mate to previous bird. Private collection.

Decorative wood ducks by Bliss. Private collection.

Merwin black duck. Copy of Wheeler. Private collection.

Pair of canvasbacks by Lou Rathmell. Private collection.

Mallard sleeper by C. R. Welles. Private collection.

Pintail drake by Charles Ralph Welles. Private collection.

Canvasback by C. R. Welles with the lines of a Laing. Private collection.

Welles black duck sleeper. Private collection.

Very light hollow-carved and feathered merganser by an unknown Stratford resident. Private collection.

Stratford scaup. Probably by Culver. Private collection.

Bliss broadbill. Private collection.

Nineteenth century Milford scaup by an unknown maker. Body sections fastened by two dowels and nails. Private collection.

Finely carved merganser, formerly the property of a Long Island museum. Now privately owned. Milford style, and attributed by some to Cassius Smith of Milford.

Red breasted merganser by Halstead Brown of Noank. Private collection.

Greater yellowlegs, Norwalk. Private collection.

Female bufflehead by Sam Collins. Shelburne Museum Collection.

American merganser drake, by Sam Collins. Shelburne Museum.

Running yellowlegs, owned by Bliss. Private collection.

Mallard drake by Tom Marshall. Private collection.

Canvasback made by Tom Marshall. Private collection.

Curlew and a pair of black breasted plovers from Southport. Maker unknown. Shelburne Museum Collection.

Feeding yellowlegs from South Norwalk. Private collection.

Willard C. Baldwin.

WILLARD C. BALDWIN (1890-1979)

Willard Clinton Baldwin was born near New Haven. At the age of nine, when his father was killed in a trolley car accident, he moved in with his grandparents in Stratford, where he lived the rest of his life. After completing high school, he got a job with the Singer Manufacturing Company in Bridgeport, commuting by trolley. He was assigned to the pattern shop and, being conscientious and skillful with his hands, he worked his way up through the shop and became manager of the pattern department, the position he held for most of his career.

As a boy, Baldwin lived next door to Shang Wheeler and was undoubtedly impressed and influenced by this prominent civic leader and sportsman who was 18 years his senior. Although he knew Wheeler and told the writer of his supplying the wood for a Wheeler goose decoy, their relationship was never as close as that between Wheeler and Bliss.

Baldwin started hunting when he was about fifteen. He bought his first shotgun from the R. B. Smith Hardware in Stratford for three dollars and fifty cents. His first rig of decoys was a mixture of factory-made and local second-hand birds.

He started carving his own decoys about 1910, making wide flat-bottomed hollow but heavy black ducks which appear to have been modeled after an old sleeper he had acquired (Page 82). Several of these earliest birds (one shown on page 82), were given to Swan Brewster about 1930 with Baldwin's statement that they were "made before I learned how to make decoys". These birds do not look much like his later ones, but close comparison does reveal common features in the head carving. Experimentation in the early years produced different styles. He developed his carving skill and by 1918 his decoys had taken on real quality. In 1923 he borrowed from "Cappy" Wicks a Holmes broadbill from which he made patterns to produce his own decoys. The contours of the bodies nearly duplicated those of Holmes. He did not use the thin bottom board, but rather a three-quarter inch board, and in many cases the seam was at the middle of the body or higher. Baldwin's broadbill heads can be distinguished from Holmes' by being less rounded, and most of them lack the "v" extension under the bill, which is characteristic of Holmes.

He later drew templates and produced copies of a Holmes black duck and a Laing goldeneye. The black ducks were made with bottom boards which varied in thickness from one-half to three-quarters inch, and the goldeneyes were constructed with the seam two inches from the bottom.

Baldwin's regular gunning decoys were black duck, broadbill, and a few goldeneyes, all of hollow

Very old sleeper owned by Willard Baldwin when he started making decoys. Possibly the model on which his first decoys were designed. Private collection.

One of Willard Baldwin's first decoys, c. 1910. Private collection.

An early high-head black duck by Willard Baldwin; atypical and probably unique. Private collection.

construction. He made one set of 20 balsa black ducks for Ralph Welles and also a small number of cork-bodied black ducks.

In his later years he shifted his efforts to decorative objects. He produced several exact copies of Laing sleeping black ducks, even to the extent of carving the "LAING" mark in the bottom—but he also put his own brand on them to show that he was not attempting deception.

Near the end of his carving career Baldwin was persuaded by his friend Harold Morse of New Rochelle, New York, to carve a variety of ducks for exhibition, though they were made with all the requisites for gunning. Since Baldwin never liked painting and Morse was a good painter, a deal was struck in which two birds each of a number of species were made. Morse painted both and kept one as his share of the project. The species included broadbill, black, mallard, goldeneye, surf scoter, red-breasted merganser, hooded merganser, wood duck and possibly others. Another friend, Mrs. John Birdseye of Trumbull, also painted a few of his black ducks.

Baldwin made no shore birds for use, but long after their killing became illegal, he did carve a few excellent decorative yellowlegs.

Willard Baldwin's decoys are characterized by careful workmanship, perfect symmetry and, except for his first ones, extremely light weight. His 1918 style of black duck, for which he is best known, was constructed from two one and one-half inch boards which, after shaping and finishing, produced a body less than three inches thick. He often used boards of different thicknesses to produce a body of a given depth. Baldwin decoys have a very "Stratford" look, with a slightly upward tilted paddle-like tail. Since many were made from Holmes patterns, they are often mistaken for Holmes', but there are differences, such as details of the head and placement of the body seam. Some of the black ducks were finished without eyes and some had eyes made from glass-headed hatpins or shoe buttons. The early scaup and goldeneyes have a yellow ring with a small cut-off black pin stuck in the center. The later more decorative birds were fitted with taxidermist's eyes.

Baldwin hunted with different men from Stratford and neighboring towns but his two closest friends and gunning companions were Kenneth Peck and Kingsley B. Hill, a prominent architect, and most of his hunting yarns involved one or the other of these men.

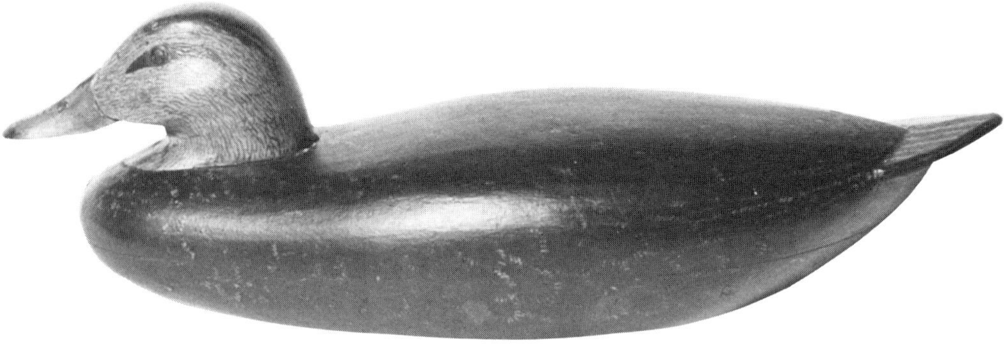

Willard Baldwin black duck of 1916. Private collection.

W. C. Baldwin black duck, the only one known with a turned head. Private collection.

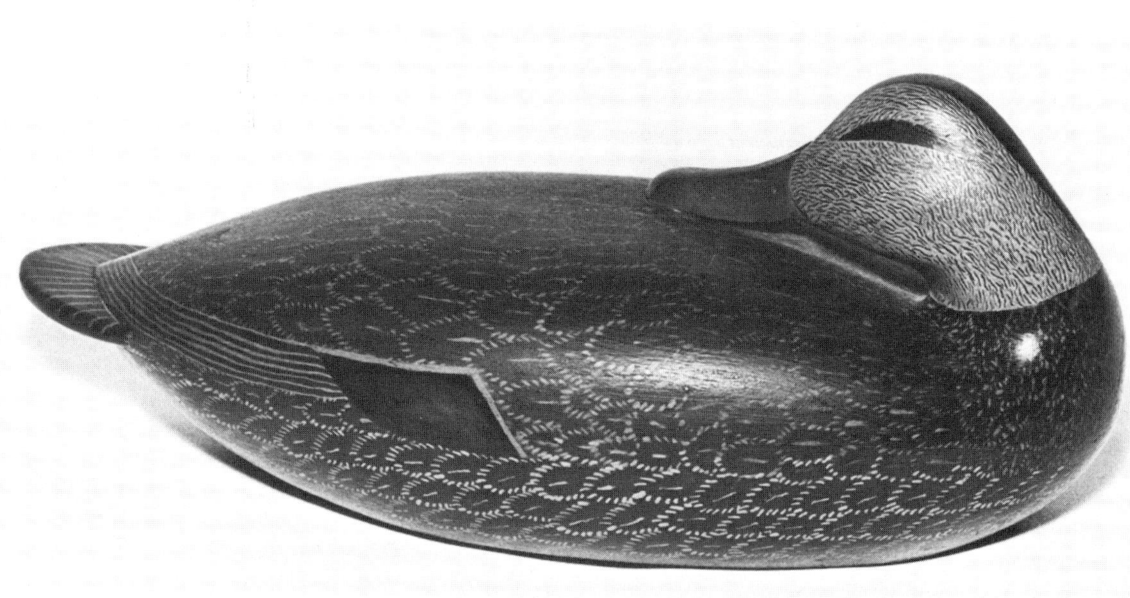

W. Baldwin copy of a Laing sleeping black duck. Private collection.

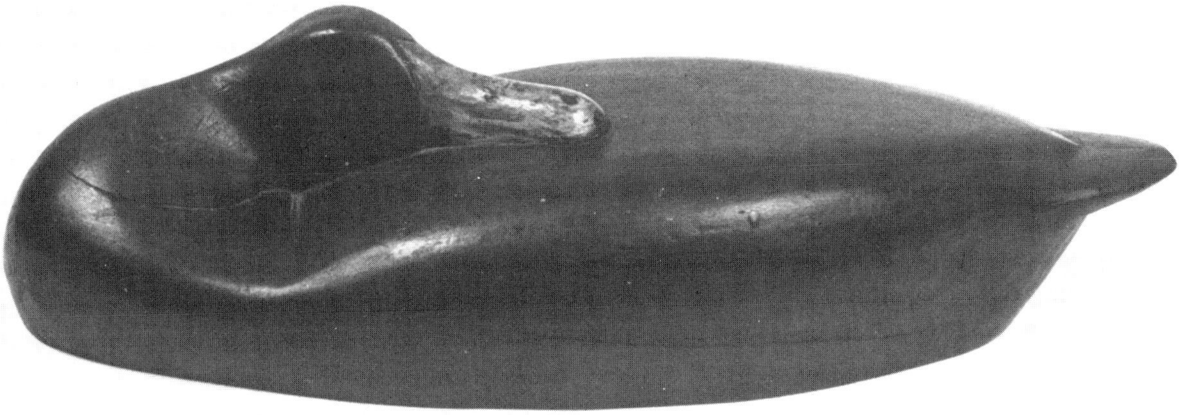

Willard Baldwin sleeping black duck. Copy of thin-bodied Laing. Collection of Ron Swanson.

Later black duck by Willard Baldwin. Private collection.

Willard Baldwin copy of Holmes black duck. A gunning decoy. Private collection.

Willard Baldwin broadbill, 1923. Private collection.

Two more Baldwin broadbills, c. 1923, showing slight variation in carving. Private collection.

Whistler by Willard Baldwin, c. 1923. Private collection.

Willard Baldwin broadbill sleeper. Private collection.

Late W. Baldwin whistler, painted by Harold Morse. Private collection.

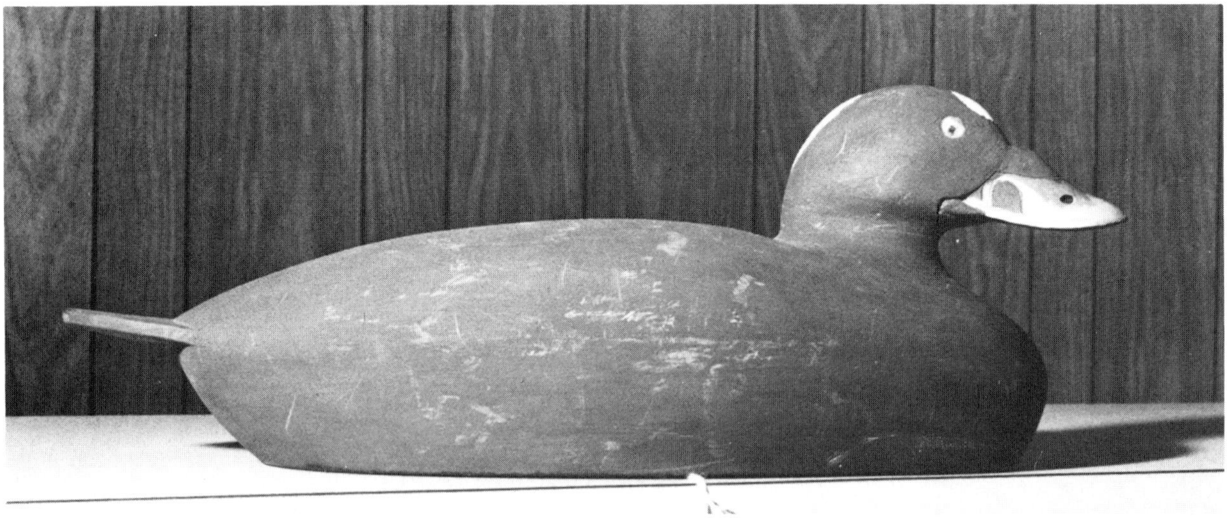

W. Baldwin surf scoter with H. Morse paint. Private collection.

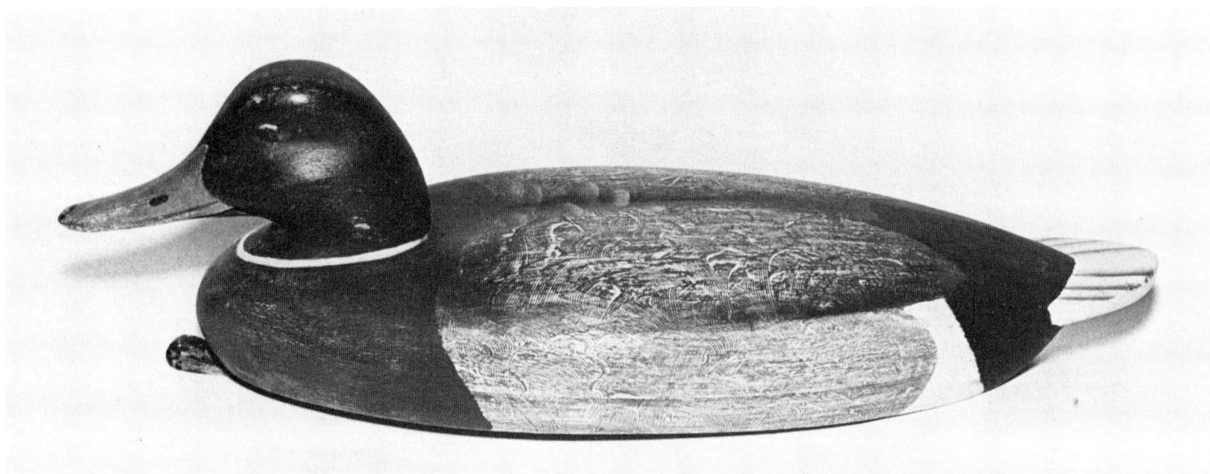

Willard Baldwin copy of Laing shallow-bodied mallard. Used by Tom Marshall. Private collection.

Wood duck by Willard Baldwin; painted by H. Morse. Private collection.

CHARLES RALPH WELLES (1895-1979)

Charles Ralph Welles, called "C R" or Ralph by his friends, was the son of Charles ("Chick") Welles who frequently hunted with Shang Wheeler. Ralph Welles's roots were deeply set in Stratford. When the old Welles house was sold after his death, the property passed from the family for the first time since it had been acquired through a royal land grant early in the seventeenth century.

Ralph Welles attended Yale University and received an engineering degree in the class of 1917. He held several industrial positions, interrupted by a term with Naval Aviation during World War II, and ended his professional career as vice president of National Steel. Though a serious businessman, he managed to find time for hunting, his favorite pastime from the age of thirteen.

For his early duck hunting he had an assortment of decoys that were very old and had been used by his father, who started hunting in the 1880s. Some of the broadbills were made by his father, and he thought others were made by Jimmy Lew Miles of Milford.

Welles started making his own decoys when he was twenty-one years old. He had come to know Shang Wheeler well, and told the writer "I copied Shang Wheeler as well as I could." His early work was so well done that it has been often mistaken for Wheeler's. The Wheeler influence is easily recognized in all of his decoys. Most often seen are broadbills and black ducks. Mallards were an extreme rarity when he first started hunting, but later he did make a few mallards plus pintails, teal, canvasbacks, and geese. These later birds included some sleepers. While all were suitably constructed for use, they seem to have been intended primarily as decoratives.

Welles's birds show good workmanship, except those made in his later years when quality deteriorated. They are hollow with the seam midway between top and bottom, or occasionally closer to the top. He attached the head with a brass screw and fastened the body sections together with glue. A slight turn to the head is common. The tails do not have the flat paddle-like shape characteristic of Stratford. They are flat on top but taper up from the rump to the tip. The bill carving is done without much detail. A distinguishing feature, especially in broadbills, is the way the underside of the bill tip is carved, with shallow indentations at the edges, suggesting but not defining a nail. Welles weights are ovoid with a rough surface. His painting was adequate but it never displayed great artistry.

The decoys he prized most highly were a string of twenty balsa black ducks made about 1923 by Willard Baldwin, whom he admired and considered a better carver than himself. Because of the tendency for the soft balsa to wear, Welles added inletted tails of pine.

As a boy, Ralph Welles hunted with his father. Later, his closest gunning friend was Donald Page. Among others he hunted with were Mead Bachelor, Shang Wheeler, Willard Baldwin, Tom Marshall, and his young nephew, Albert L. Worthen, Jr. He hunted the Connecticut River as well as the Housatonic, and made several hunting trips to the Great Lakes.

Welles spent his active life in Stratford but traveled a lot for his company. After retiring from National Steel, he worked as a real estate broker for a few years in New Rochelle, New York, and then moved to Ivoryton, Connecticut, where he lived most of the final years before his death in 1979 in a Stamford nursing home.

C. R. Welles broadbill, Wheeler pattern. Private collection.

Early Welles scaup, probably 1920s. Private collection.

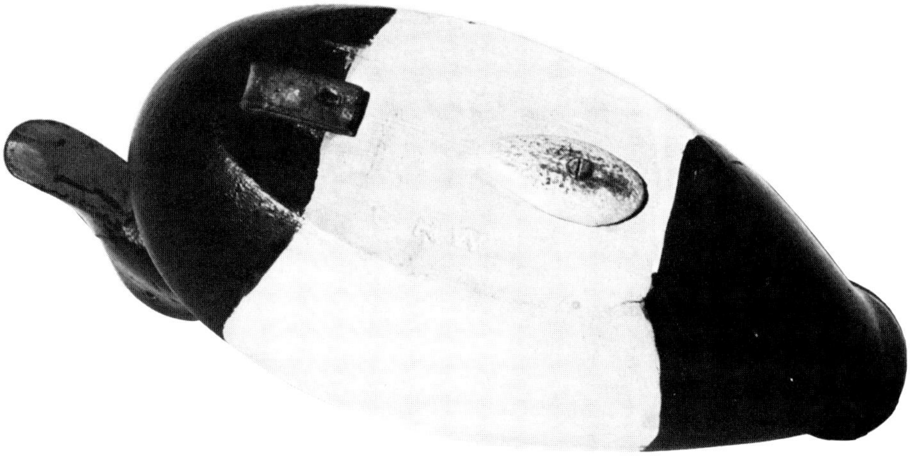

Bottom of Welles scaup showing brand and typical weight. Notice also carving pattern under bill.

Welles black duck. Private collection.

Welles black duck in Wheeler style. Private collection.

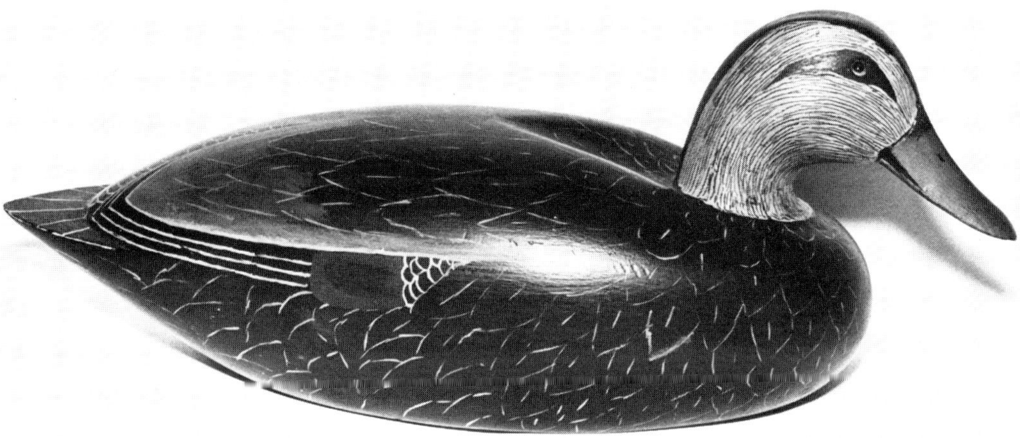

Welles black duck. A later style. Private collection.

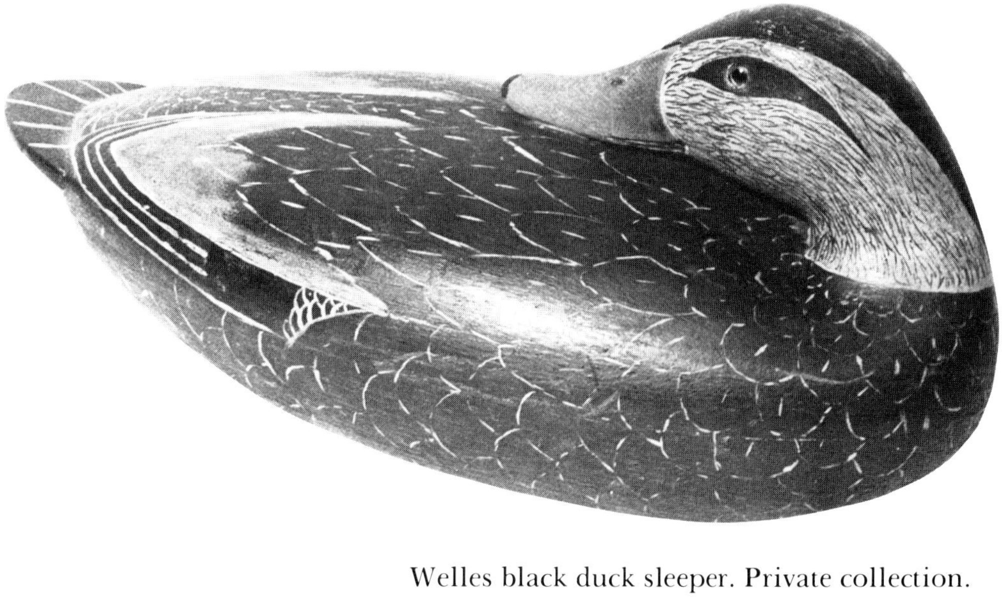

Welles black duck sleeper. Private collection.

Pair of late Welles broadbills, 1960s. Quality had deteriorated. Private collection.

Welles mallard drake. Private collection.

Reginald I. Culver.

REGINALD IRVING CULVER (1897-1975)

Reginald I. Culver, a native of Stratford, was the son of Bob Culver, a steamboat captain. At age fifteen, Reginald became an apprentice pattern maker with the well-known decoy carver, Roswell Bliss, who probably stimulated his interest in making decoys.

After three years with Bliss, Culver became a pattern maker for O. S. Platt in Bridgeport, and after another three years, at the start of the first World War, he enlisted in the Navy where he served on the battleships North Carolina and Arkansas. While with the Navy in San Francisco in 1920 he made a rig of 15 broadbills.

On returning to Stratford in 1922, he worked as a carpenter and at a variety of jobs on and near the water, such as shelling, oystering, and sailing as a hand on his father's steamer, "Stratford." He acquired a pilot's license and a master's license. At various times he worked for Shang Wheeler's Stratford Oyster Company, the Moran Towing Company, and Sikorsky Aircraft. He retired from the last company in 1962 and continued to live in Stratford until his death thirteen years later.

Culver had an excellent start in decoy making, for in the same year that he started work with Bliss, Ben Holmes died and Reg Culver bought Holmes' unfinished blocks from his widow. There were 70 in the lot, all broadbills. He completed construction of these decoys with heads of his own design. The use of Holmes bodies has led to confusion and to false attribution of many Culver broadbills to Holmes. Culver heads can be distinguished from Holmes' by being flat on top, having low bulging cheeks and thinner necks. The bodies made entirely by Culver were blockier and less graceful than those begun by Holmes. All of his black duck bodies were of his own design, constructed from a three-inch board of sugar pine or cedar, which was hollowed and fitted with a five-eighths inch, three-quarter inch, or one inch bottom board. The breasts of Culver's decoys have a pronounced inward slant.

Though some of Culver's carving details seem to be consistent, there is great variation in the shape of the heads. The dimensions and shape of the head and bill differ so widely among individuals that they often appear to have had different makers.

Culver made mostly straight-headed broadbills and black ducks and a few goldeneyes, as well as a small number of scoter sleepers, all of the Holmes-type bottom-board construction. He made also a few black ducks and scoters of cork. He used, in addition to decoys of his own make, a motley collection of both solid and hollow decoys by other makers from the area. Some had been made by his father, Captain Bob, and others had been owned by him. Reginald Culver branded most of the decoys he made or used "R. I. CULVER." Some of his decoys were sold or given to friends, but the entire lot in his possession in 1959, 135 in all, were sold by Culver to Bill Mackey for $500.

A wide variety of Stratford decoys are seen with Culver heads. The explanation for this fact is that Culver repaired many decoys for himself and other owners, and he also sold separate heads.

Culver scaup. Courtesy of Bourne Gallery.

Reginald I. Culver black duck. Private collection.

Comparison of Holmes and Culver black ducks. Holmes in rear.

Culver scaup with an unusually slanted breast. Private collection.

Scaup with a Culver head. Body also probably by Culver. Private collection.

Black duck sleeper by Reginald Culver. Private collection.

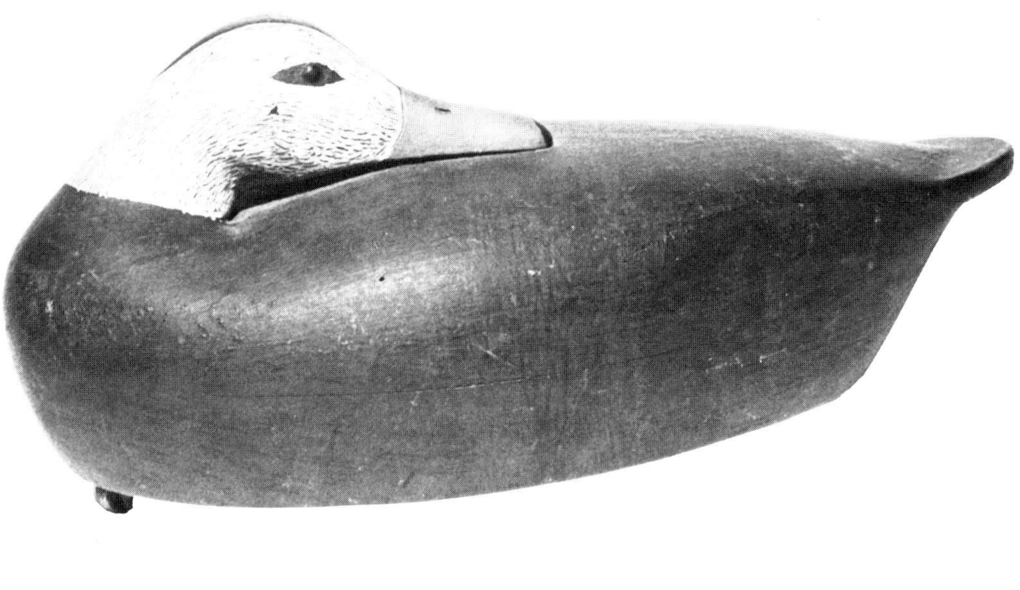

Lou Rathmell, foreground, with Bill Bedell on the East breakwater, off Bridgeport.

LOUIS C. RATHMELL (1898-1974)

Lou Rathmell was an outstanding sportsman and a great competitor. He made an effort to excel at everything he undertook and usually succeeded. He was the most famous fisherman, a renowned rod-maker, the best shot, and one of the best decoy makers ever known to the sportsmen of Stratford. In quality, versatility, and decoy style, Shang Wheeler was the master. However, for working black ducks, Rathmell is considered by many to have been his equal.

Louis C. Rathmell was born in Ocean Grove, New Jersey, son of an ardent hunter and fisherman. He lived for much of his boyhood in Asbury Park but spent most of his adult life in Danbury, Connecticut, working as an oil salesman for the Texaco Company. His magnificent home, on the second highest hill in town, was referred to locally as "The Castle". Of Polish descent, Rathmell was a man of medium height, with blond hair, an asset which made him look very young for his years. Though he lived in Danbury, he spent his leisure hours fishing in Long Island Sound and hunting around Stratford, especially at Knell's Island. He hunted regularly with Frank Novak.

Rathmell's first gunning for ducks in Knell's Island was over very crude rough-bodied cork decoys. A fellow hunter once described the heads "atrocious." Whether these decoys were made by Rathmell, or by another, is not known, but the derision he received for their lack of quality challenged him to make a set that would be admired by both man and duck. This was in the mid-thirties. Rathmell became so successful in producing handsome decoys that they were often mistaken for Wheeler's. He used "Fibracork" for bodies. All had wooden tails, and on some he attached wooden bottoms for extra durability. Rectangular weights were inletted and often stamped with his name and date of manufacture. The only

Lou Rathmell black duck from Tom Marshall's hunting rig. Before 1941. Private collection.

Black duck from Lou Rathmell's famous 1941 flock. Private collection.

adverse criticism the writer has heard is that a Rathmell duck appears pinched at the base of the bill, best described by a non-admiring collector as "like a Wheeler with its dentures out"!

Rathell's most famous rig of forty black ducks was made and dated 1941. The carving and careful scratch painting of the heads are especially noteworthy. Each head was carved and mounted with its own special attitude of turn or tilt, so that no two are alike. They made a most impressive realistic flock of ducks. Each member seems to transmit a personality as though it were alive.

After proving to his colleagues that he could make a fine decoy, Rathmell decided to enter competition in the national shows. He won many prizes with his exhibition quality hollow-carved wood decoys.

When he was about sixty, Rathmell started developing cataracts and had to give up hunting. He continued carving for a while but had lost the delicate touch of an artist and the product of his later efforts lacked beauty. Fishing now became his major sporting activity. He built his own fishing boats and made his own rods and lures. In 1973 at age 75, the year before his death, he was credited with catching with rod and reel 400 blue fish and 1300 stripers, some weighing over fifty pounds.

At the peak of his shooting career, Lou Rathmell had an enviable reputation for five-shot bags. As a flight was hitting the water he would shoot the last duck while still in the air, then take them one at a time as they rose again. He seldom missed or crippled a bird.

Another 1941 Rathmell black duck. Private collection.

Rathmell 1941 black duck with tucked down head. Private collection.

Detail of tucked-head Rathmell.

Rathmell black duck with bill submerged, in sleeping position. Private collection.

Bottom of Rathmell black duck, showing inletted weight with date and name.

Rathmell black duck with head turned completely back. Though called a sleeper, he looks pretty alert! Private collection.

Rathmell hollow-carved mallard drake. Private collection.

Rathmell mallard duck. Private collection.

Exhibition grade broadbills by Lou Rathmell. Private collection.

Canvasbacks. Rathmell exhibition birds. Private collection.

CHARLES R. DISBROW (1885-1955)

Charles Disbrow was born and brought up in Stratford, and he grew up and became a state game warden. His father was an Army general who finished out his military career as the Commandant of Weston Academy, a local military school in Weston, Connecticut, which incidentally, Shang Wheeler attended.

During his early years, Disbrow did most of his hunting behind his house on Peacock Creek. He also hunted along the Housatonic River, just east of his home. His first decoys were factory made, but he soon started making his own, of both cork and wood. All were rather large and those of wood were heavy, being made from two or three boards nailed together with little or no hollowing. The heads were large and thick with short heavy necks, very long straight bills, and glass eyes. Spoon-cast lead weights were used. Disbrow's early birds were judged as "pretty bad" by his peers.

Disbrow was a friend of Wheeler and asked for his help in improving the quality of his own carving. As a result of Wheeler's guidance, the results were some fine-looking birds, close enough in appearance to often be mistaken for Wheelers. The black duck in Johnsgard's *The Bird Decoy* identified as a Shang Wheeler is in actuality a Charles Disbrow that had been given by Disbrow to Tom Marshall for his collection. Certainly the understandable mislabel is a tribute to Disbrow's ability. The ultimate tribute to Disbrow's skill as a carver came in the 1951 North American Decoy Makers Contest when he won first place for his black duck in the amateur division. Lou Rathmell of Danbury, Connecticut came in second.

The transition from "clunkers" to fine Wheeler style black ducks appears to have been made in stages, rather than by a single jump. Some birds with bodies like his best are fitted with less carefully carved heads, better than but reminiscent of some of his early work.

In comparing a Wheeler and a Disbrow, it will be seen that the Disbrow is a chunkier, slightly less graceful bird that doesn't quite have the sleek shape of a true Wheeler. Disbrow's heads are carefully carved, but they lack the lifelike quality of a Wheeler or Rathmell, partly because the eyes are usually placed too far back and too low. In even his last birds, with detailed carving under the bills, he somehow missed the proper detail of the head-to-bill joint.

There is a group of multilayered, heavy-billed, well-carved decoys from Milford which some collectors have attributed to Disbrow. A good many scaup pairs and at least one greenwing teal are known. The complete lack of similarity in features between these birds and of Disbrow's early or later work has led the writer to question that they were made by Disbrow, even though there is evidence that he owned some of them.

Early black duck by Charles Disbrow. Private collection.

Disbrow black duck. Intermediate style. Private collection.

Disbrow black duck. More refined style. Private collection.

Disbrow black duck of last and best form. Private collection.

Disbrow black duck. His best attempt to copy Wheeler. This bird, unlike the previous examples, has a turned head. Private collection.

Scaup with features strongly reminiscent of Disbrow's early work. Possibly made by him. Private collection.

Multi-layered hollow-carved scaup in original paint. From Milford; attributed to Charles Disbrow. Private collection.

A mate to previous bird. Though these birds have for many years been attributed to Disbrow, the attribution is questioned. Private collection.

Multi-layered hollow green-winged teal drake by same maker as scaup above. Private collection.

Tom Marshall in his living room.

THOMAS CARVER MARSHALL (1903-1983)

Thomas C. Marshall was born in West Newton, Massachusetts, and completed his formal schooling at Worcester Academy. Very early in life he developed a fascination for woods and waters and wildlife. Before he was old enough to carry a gun, he accompanied his grandfather on partridge hunting trips. In his *Leads to Knell's Island* (publication pending) he relates the pleasure of being in the woods on crisp sunny fall days with the old man, of savoring the delicious lunches they carried, and of gathering chestnuts among the fallen leaves. He also describes in detail the exciting experiences he had in his teens, with several other boys, operating a goose gunning blind at Scituate, Massachusetts, using live decoys.

Marshall moved to Connecticut in 1927 and went to work for Remington Arms after that company bought out his father's insulation business, with which he was associated. His professional career was with various manufacturing concerns, where he held responsible positions in production and sales. As a final profession, he ran his own management consulting firm. He had two happy marriages and one son. His second wife, Betty, shared his love for the out-of-doors and hunted ducks and rails and upland game with him.

Shortly after moving to Connecticut, Marshall met and became a good friend of Kenneth Peck, who taught him the ways of ducks and how to hunt them on Knell's Island. He was also befriended by Shang Wheeler, who got him started in the proper fashion with a good string of decoys—Laings, Holmes, and others—to replace his first ones from Pascagoula, Mississippi, that Wheeler thought were of poor quality.

Marshall, more than anyone before him, appreciated the greatness of Albert Laing as a carver. He acquired Laing's gunning journal from the Beers family who bought Laing's house. At one time his gunning rig contained more Laing birds than were owned by any other individual.

Marshall's favorite gunning spots were Knell's Island and the New Haven breakwater. At the former, as well as other areas, he also hunted rail, and was a devotee of this sport. He kept prize-winning retrievers that were specially trained for rail, and was a founder of the Irish Water Spaniel Club.

An active conservationist, Marshall was a Field Representative for Ducks Unlimited and Chairman of the Connecticut Audubon Society's Birdcraft Museum in Fairfield. He led the campaign to have the State take over and manage Knell's Island as The Charles E. Wheeler Wildlife Area.

Cork-bodied whistler by Tom Marshall in the style of Wheeler. Private collection.

Balsa white-winged scoter. One of the best decoys hand-made by Tom Marshall. Private collection.

The New York Decoy Makers Contests that began in Bellport moved to Grand Central Palace, became national in scope, and attracted carvers from all over the country. These shows, that gave impetus to carving and collecting, were directed by Tom Marshall for their life span of five years. It was at the first show in 1947 that Shang Wheeler became nationally recognized as the outstanding decoy carver of his day.

Besides the first string of decoys received from Wheeler, Tom Marshall shot over many other fine decoys. Wheeler gave him a set of twelve cork full-bodies black ducks, and he used many Bliss scaup and a few Rathmell black ducks. After he sold his true Laing and Holmes birds, he had Laing replicas made to replace the originals. They are black ducks and scaup, both straight-heads and sleepers, lathe-turned from patterns made by Willard Baldwin. A few replicas of other species, copies of Wheeler and Holmes, were also used.

Marshall started making decoys soon after moving to Connecticut. Many were of his own design and others, with more artistic merit, were modeled after Wheeler. He made hollow pine black ducks, mallards, canvasbacks, goldeneyes, buffleheads, and widgeon, cork composite goldeneyes, and balsa scoters, as well as a few decoratives. His carving skill was best demonstrated in the excellent lifelike decorative shore birds that he made for fund-raising auctions at the annual dinners of the Fairfield chapter of Ducks Unlimited.

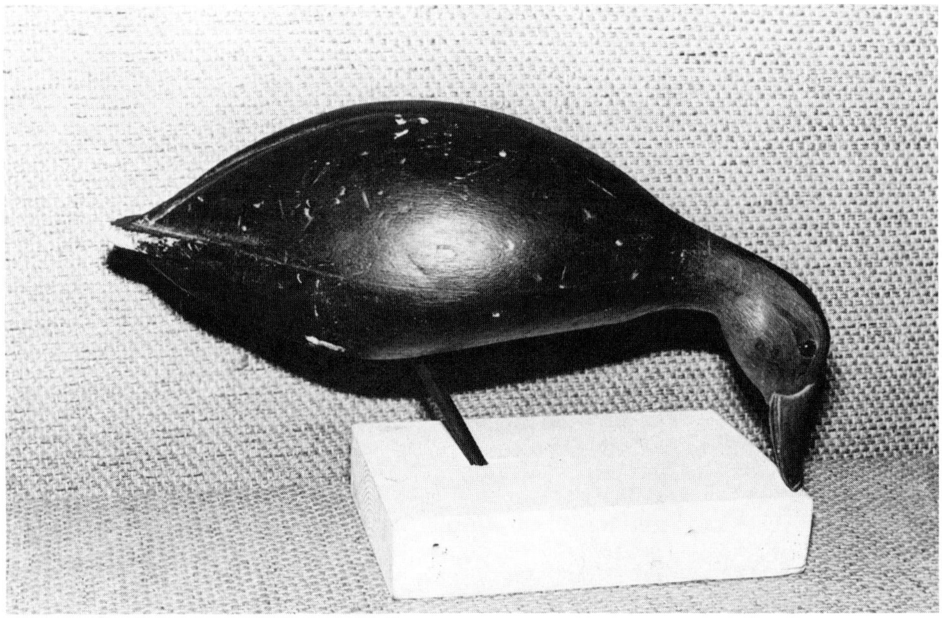

Balsa stick-up feeder black duck by Tom Marshall. Private collection.

Gunning decoys of Tom Marshall. The patterns were made by Baldwin, copying Laings. They were then reproduced on lathes, and the finishing and painting was done by Marshall. Private collection.

Copy of a Laing black duck from a pattern by Baldwin. Factory turned. Hollowing, finishing, and painting by Marshall. Private collection.

Working scoter in the style of Wheeler. Joint design of Marshall and Gleason, factory reproduced, and finished by Gleason. Private collection.

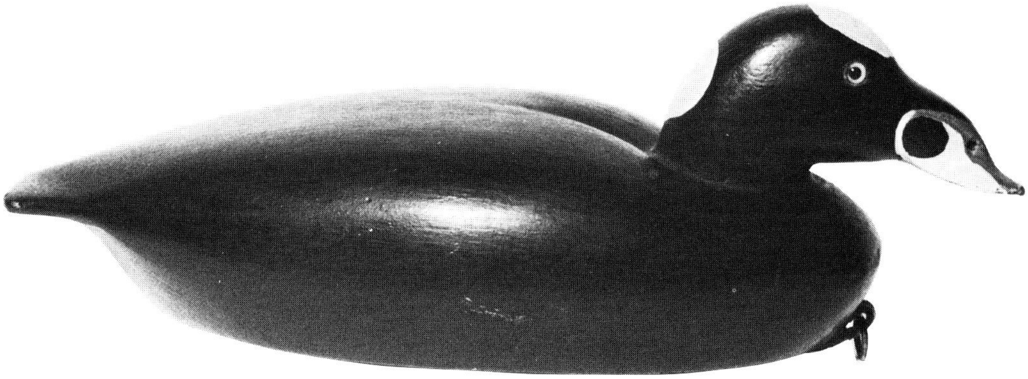

Hollow-carved mallard hen by Tom Marshall. Private collection.

Hollow wood bufflehead by Tom Marshall. Private collection.

Working goldeneye. Design by Gleason, factory reproduced, and finished for use by Tom Marshall (never used). Private collection.

Kenneth Peck pointing to the sign on his Stratford house that was built in 1740.

KENNETH BIRDSEY PECK (1887-1961)

Kenneth B. Peck was born in Stratford in 1887, the only son of a lawyer, Charles Peck, who became a well-known judge. Ken went to high school, but never had much interest in books. His great love as a young man was the out-of-doors and especially the water, and for the rest of his life that's where he made his living.

In his early days he earned extra money from the sea and coastline, catching stripers and bluefish, crabs, oysters and clams, and in the fall, shooting and selling black ducks. For a while he was hired by Cappy Wicks, a market shooter and guide. As he got older, Peck became a pleasure boat captain, skippering well-known boats of the time, including the "Discovery", a schooner owned by DeVer Warner, a Bridgeport industrialist. He also sailed as chief cook on boats of Horace Merwin, a Bridgeport banker.

Ken Peck hunted over a rig of decoys that would make any collector burn with envy—black ducks and broadbills made by Laing, Holmes, Baldwin, Bliss, and others. He made a few decoys for himself over the years, of cork and wood. His best known are a rig of black ducks, made in 1933, with his friend, Bill Bedell. They have typical Stratford style hollow-carved bodies made from two-inch boards. Peck didn't believe in fancy painting. The birds are purely functional, clean and crisply made, with black bodies and scratch-painted heads and glass eyes. The weights are pointed tear-drops, heavier than the average Stratford weights, and have flat rather than rounded edges. The leather anchor loops are secured by brass screws.

Peck and Bedell worked together, neither one following a rigid pattern in carving heads. All of the heads face directly forward, but there is great variation in their appearance. The product of this effort has been reported to be 50 decoys, 25 by Peck and 25 by Bedell. Most of the Bedell birds have been accounted for, but only two with Peck's signature are known. It is probably inaccurate to attribute any single decoy from the lot solely to one man or the other.

Ken Peck or "Pecky", as his friends called him, was a jovial man who was well-liked and respected by his peers as the ultimate in duck hunters. He hunted regularly with Bill Bedell and Willard Baldwin, and was also a friend of Tom Marshall, who said he learned all he knew about duck shooting from Ken Peck. Willard Baldwin once remarked, "He was one of the finest gunners Stratford has ever seen."

Peck was one of the few people of his time who had any interest in the source and history of decoys. Shortly before his death, he stamped his attribution on the birds in his possession, about 150 in all, made up of many by Willard Baldwin, Bliss, and Arthur Baldwin, and lesser numbers by other Stratford makers such as Ben Holmes, and one each by Laing, Wheeler, John Hanford, and Bill Lattin. All of the older birds had in-use repaint, expertly done on the scaup and goldeneyes, but with a non-glare sand-filled brown on the bodies of most of the blacks. Some of the very old birds had been reheaded.

Ken Peck black duck, 1933. Private collection.

Bottom view of Ken Peck black duck, showing his stamping, weight, and holding strap. Private collection.

WILLIAM EDWARD BEDELL III (1904-1960)

William Bedell was a graduate of Norwich University where he was a star basketball player. He worked as manager of the painting department in his father's shipyard in Stratford. The Bedell shipyard had a large sail loft with sliding doors on the southeast end, overlooking the Knell's Island marsh. From that high vantage point, Bill Bedell could see where every duck entering the marsh set down and also spot where each of the hunters was hiding out. With an edge like that, he almost always had good shooting. He hunted with Ken Peck, Bob Culver, Lou Rathmell, Ralph Welles, and Tom Marshall.

In 1933 Bedell made up a rig of 25 black duck decoys, in partnership with Ken Peck, described previously.

Black duck made by Bill Bedell in 1933. Private collection.

Bill Bedell 1933 black duck. Private collection.

WILLIAM V. LATTIN (-1934)

Little is known about William V. Lattin except that he lived in Stratford and worked for the New Haven Railroad. He was making excellent broadbill and black duck decoys in 1890. The bodies are similar to Holmes', but more angular, and the tails of both species are flat and squared off at the ends. The uniformity of carving and paint of the broadbills, that were made with two different head forms, gives the impression that they were factory-produced. Some still exist in original nearly unused condition. Distinguishing features are the initials "W V L", stamped on the bottom and an unusual boat-like form of lead weight.

William V. Lattin scaup. Original paint, c. 1890. Private collection.

William V. Lattin scaup, with head carving different from previous bird. (Both are original.) Private collection.

Bottom of Lattin scaup showing detail of tail carving and typical Lattin weight.

William V. Lattin black duck, c. 1890. Private collection.

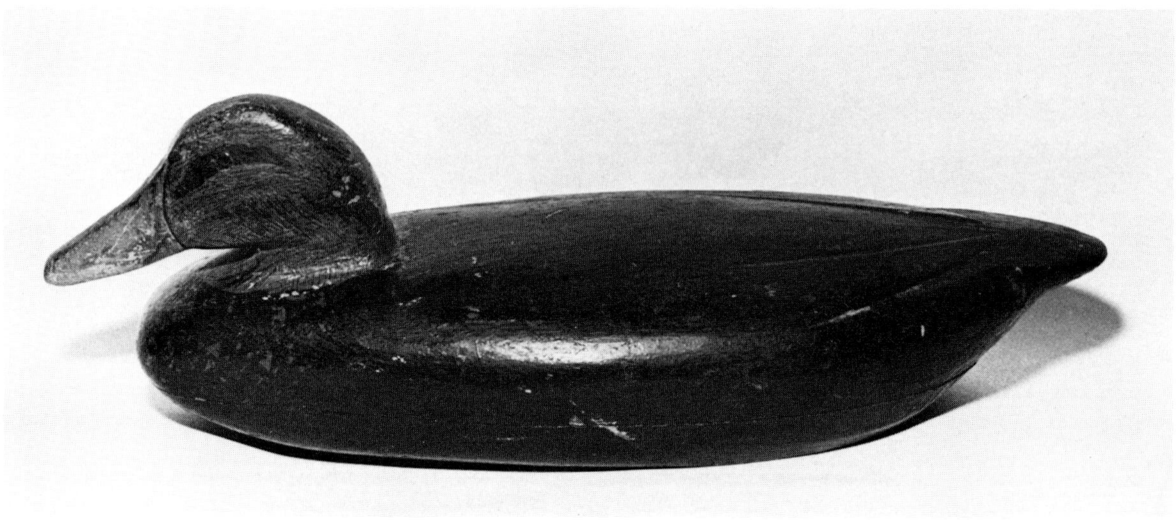

Swan Brewster black duck from the first rig he made—1920s. Private collection.

SWAN BREWSTER (1899-)

Swan Brewster was born in Stratford in 1899 and spent most of his life there and in the adjoining town of Bridgeport, where he held various positions with the General Electric Company. He started hunting when he was nine.

Willard Baldwin gave Brewster his first decoys, some that Baldwin had made about 1910. They were wide heavy-bodied black ducks. Brewster continued to use these decoys, but began supplementing them with decoys of his own make about 1920. They were hollow and thin-bodied, apparently hand-made without use of patterns, for no two were identical. There were differences in body thickness and in the location of the seam between the upper and lower sections. On some he carved slightly raised wing tips. The heads, though varied in shape, seemed to have been modeled on the Baldwin style and pointed straight forward. His black ducks and the thicker-bodied broadbills, made later, can be recognized as Stratford birds, but they are crudely fashioned and lack the eye-pleasing balance and quality of a later Baldwin or Bliss.

Swan Brewster was not a member of the group of Stratford gunners of his day who knew each other well and hunted together regularly. He was a loner and he hunted less frequently than the rest. He made decoys only for his own use during his Stratford years.

After retirement, Brewster moved with his wife up to West Shokan, New York, in the Catskills. At 88 he was still hunting upland game birds and fishing for trout. His skill as a carver improved over the years, and he used it in carving decorative ducks and other birds and fish. His sleeping teal are especially attractive.

HORACE B. MERWIN (1888-1947)

Horace Merwin, a Fairfield banker and wealthy sportsman, was a friend of Wheeler and his most skillful imitator. He made exhibition grade decoys that were almost indistinguishable from Wheelers.

Horace B. Merwin black duck; copy of Wheeler. Private collection.

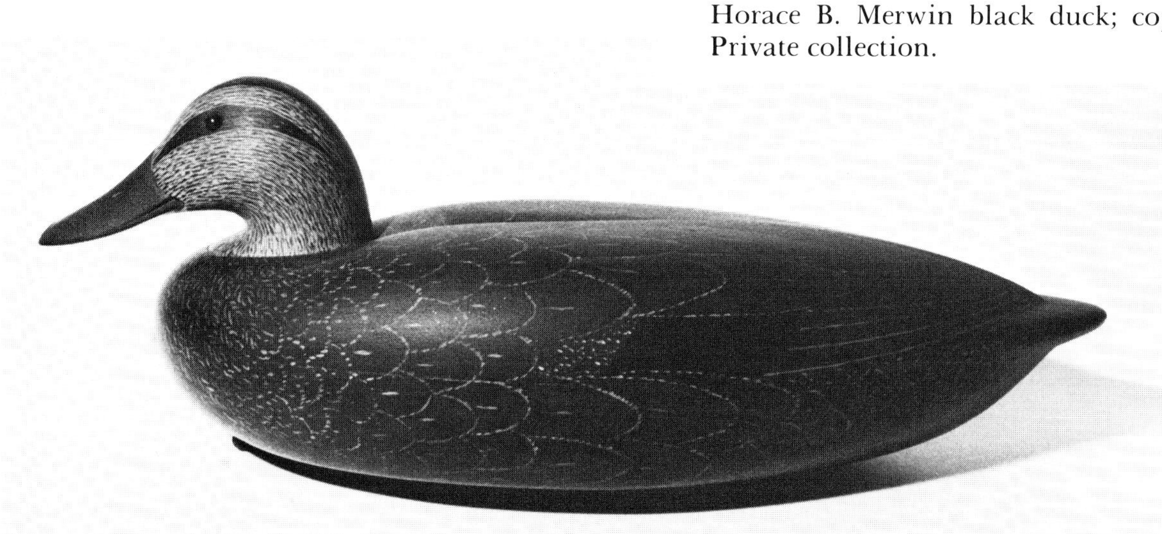

Merwin black duck; copy of Holmes style. Private collection.

Merwin sleeper in style of Wheeler. Private collection.

Cork-bodied scaup drake by Horace Merwin. Private collection.

Merwin white-winged scoter. An exact copy of Wheeler. Private collection.

Merwin scaup duck. Private collection.

Horace Merwin goldeneye; Wheeler pattern. Private collection.

ARTHUR CLAYTON (1911-1974)

Arthur Clayton was a native of England who moved with his family to Bridgeport, Connecticut, at the age of three. For most of his adult life he lived in the adjoining town of Fairfield. He was president of the Clayton Press printing company.

Clayton excelled at many sports—golf, hockey, figure skating—and was a sports fisherman and hunter. He was hunting by the time he was twelve, and started carving decoys in his mid-twenties. He made 25-30 working decoys, mostly black ducks and broadbills. During the early 1940s he carved competition grade decoys and entered them in the National Decoy contests in New York City, where he won several ribbons, including a few blues.

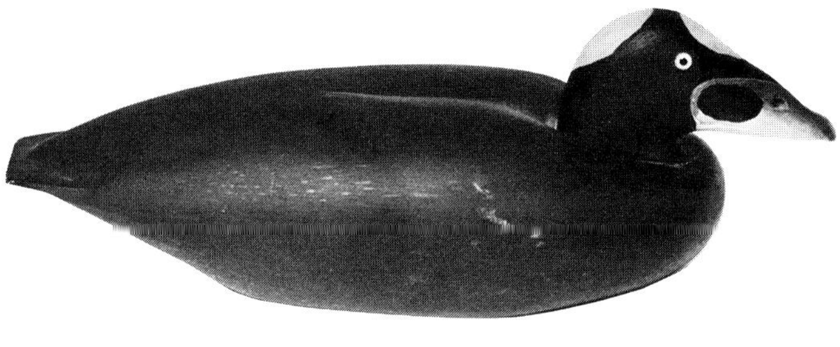

Arthur Clayton surf scoter. A copy of Wheeler. Private collection.

Arthur Clayton scaup drake. Note almost exact duplication of Wheeler scaup. Private collection.

ARTHUR CHACE

Arthur Chace of Fairfield is a retired business executive and a former president of Ducks Unlimited. He hunted with a syndicate organized by William Rudkin of Fairfield and others at Langford Creek, Maryland with local decoys. In Connecticut he used oversized black ducks by Ralf Coykendall, as well as several racks of broadbill and scoter silhouettes totalling 120 made by himself, with help from a son.

OTHER STRATFORD MAKERS

Stratford produced many lesser decoy makers, with varying degrees of skill. Reginald Culver's father, Captain Bob, and his cousin, Irving, made a few mediocre decoys. Other makers of the late nineteenth and early twentieth century were John Hanford, Walter Hubbell, and Byron Romer. Two carvers who made only a small number of black ducks in imitation of Wheeler were William Russell Breit and William Bentley. Breit's birds are handsome; he followed Wheeler's pattern closely, except for the bills that are too straight. Bentley was less of a craftsman. His heads are too thick and the bills not well formed. For the one sleeper he constructed, according to his wife, he had to call on Wheeler for help.

There are still a few hunters here who make their own decoys but, as elsewhere in the State, those with artistic talent now concentrate their efforts on decoratives.

Walter Hubbell of Stratford—black. Private collection.

Irving Culver black duck. Private collection.

Broadbill attributed to Byron Romer. Private collection.

Black duck by William Russell Breit of Stratford, a Wheeler imitator. Private collection.

William Bentley black duck. Private collection.

Broadbill from the gunning rig of C. R. Welles, of Stratford. He thought this bird might have been made by Jimmy Lou Miles. Private collection.

A broadbill from C. R. Welles, who said he thought it was made by his father. Private collection.

A graceful broadbill with slightly inletted head. Maker uncertain, though it could have been Ben Holmes or Willard Baldwin. Workmanship is better than typical examples of either. Private collection.

Early bottom-board whistler, possibly by Laing. The bowed-up breast and the deep body curvature where the head is attached are typically Laing. Private collection.

Very old Stratford scaup owned by Arthur Baldwin. Possibly an Early Laing or early Holmes, or the prototype of Holmes broadbills. Private collection.

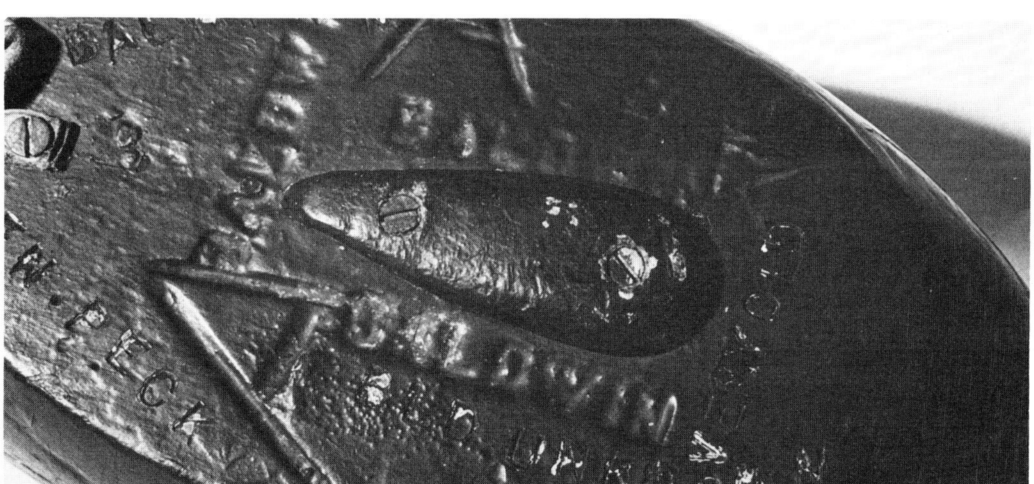

Bottom of previous bird. Showing "BALDWIN" brands and carving, and information stamped on by Ken Peck. Private collection.

Old squaw attributed to Laing. This appears to be the model used by Wheeler and Bliss for their old squaws. Private collection.

Bottom of old squaw attributed to Laing, showing brands of Baldwin and Bliss.

Old squaw; brother to previous bird. Bottom-board construction. Shelburne Museum.

Whistler by same maker as old squaws. With bottom-board, as in earliest hollow Laing black ducks. Shelburne Museum.

Unknown Stratford scaup with Laing and Holmes features. Midseam construction. Shelburne Museum.

Old squaw by an unknown maker. Acquired in 1903 by Ken Peck, who guessed that it was made between 1860 and 1890. Private collection.

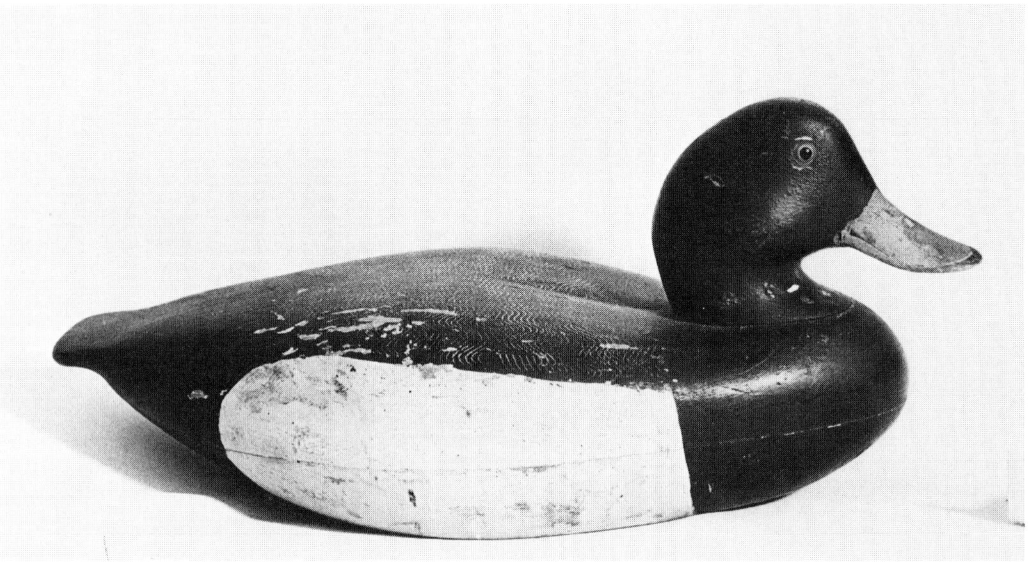

Stratford scaup with a body by an unknown maker and head by Benjamin Holmes. Private collection.

Early solid broadbill from Stratford. Unknown maker. Private collection.

Very early canvasback from the Stratford area. Solid construction. Maker unknown. Private collection.

Very early old squaw from Stratford. Not of the "Stratford" style. The bill has been replaced. Private collection.

A folksy solid broadbill found in Stratford. Maker unknown, probably of the 19th century. Private collection.

Ruddy duck of solid construction, from Stratford. A very rare species for a Connecticut decoy. Private collection.

A very old hollow-carved old squaw or ruddy duck of an unknown maker's individual design and paint pattern. Found in Stratford. Private collection.

Scaup attributed to J. W. Selleck. Swanson collection.

Crude early unknown black duck. Branded "S.B. Wheeler". Private collection.

Unknown Stratford broadbill. Private collection.

Unknown Stratford broadbill. Courtesy Wm. Doyle Galleries.

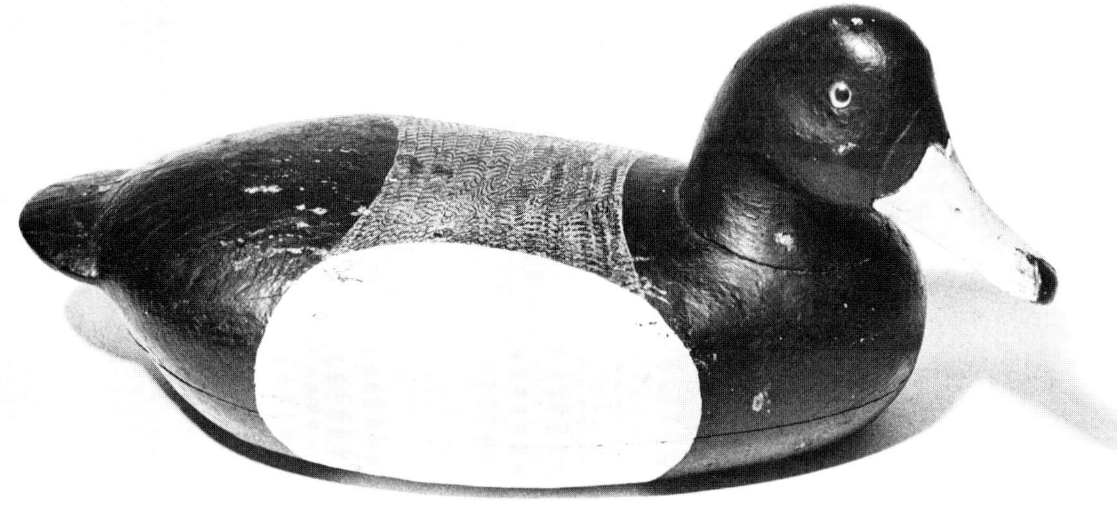

Unknown Stratford broadbill owned and branded by Reginald Culver. Private collection.

Bottom of broadbill, showing Culver brand.

Unknown Stratford scaup. From Tom Marshall's first rig acquired from Wheeler. Private collection.

Three-layered scaup by unknown. Stratford maker. Private collection.

Cousin to preceding broadbill. Same maker. Private collection.

Broadbill branded "I. MEACHEN". Private collection.

Unknown old black duck owned by Cappy Wicks. Same maker as Stratford unknown "I. MEACHEN" broadbill. Private collection.

Scoter by an unknown Stratford carver. Private collection.

Stratford scoter. Maker unknown. Shelburne Museum.

A fine very old hollow-carved black by an unknown Stratford maker. Possibly an early Wheeler. Private collection.

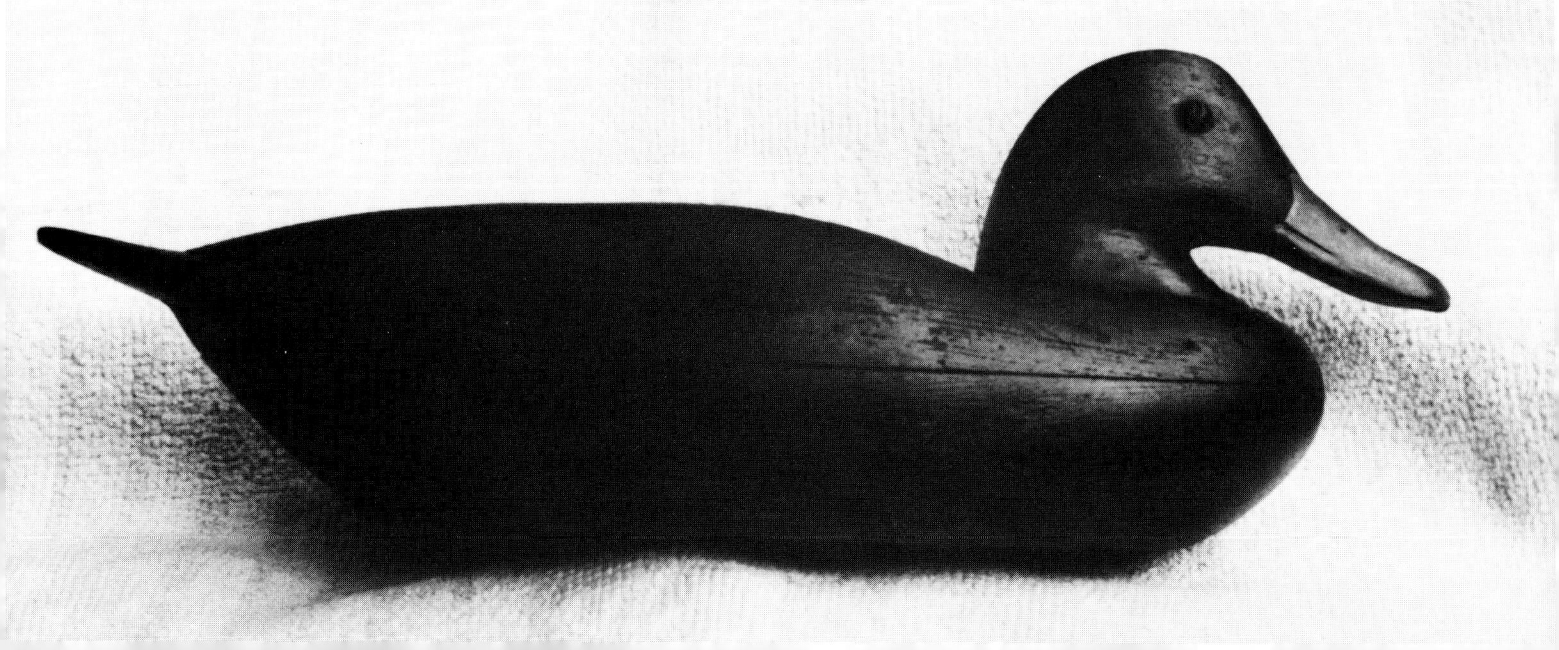

Feather-carved black duck by unknown maker from Stratford. Private collection.

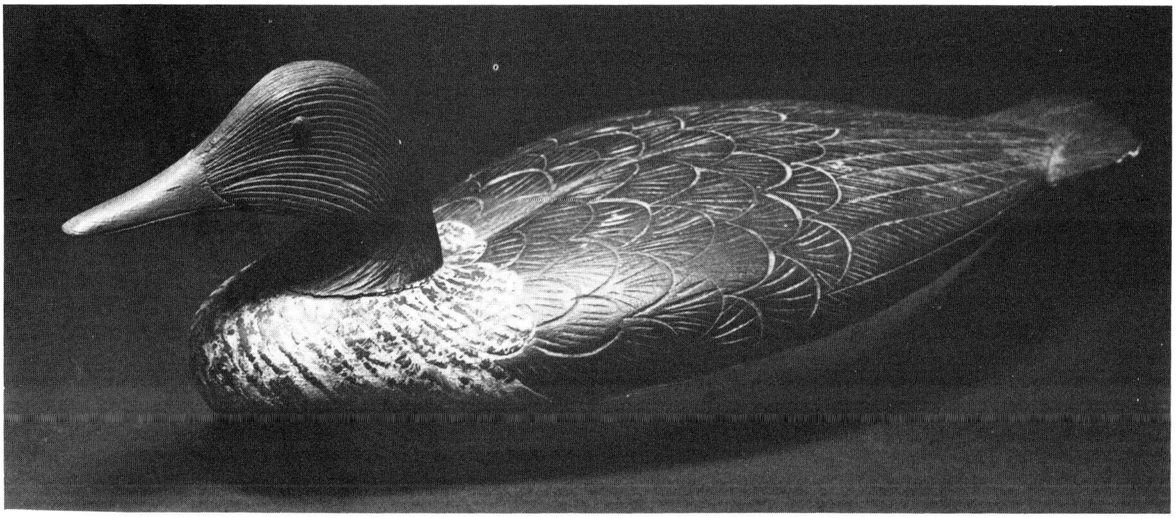

A merganser by same maker as previous bird. Private collection.

Early Stratford black ducks—maker unknown. Found in same rig as several thin-bodied Laings. Courtesy Wm. Doyle Galleries.

Hollow-carved widgeon by an early unknown Housatonic River maker. Private collection.

MILFORD DECOYS

At about the same time that Laing's decoys were setting the style for local gunners, another style was also developing in the area, on the Milford side of the Housatonic River. These birds, designated as "Milford" decoys, were of hollow construction like the Laings, but of chunkier build and with shorter tails. They were made with high breasts to ride the waves in the same manner as their Stratford cousins. The distinguishing difference is in the shape of the body. It is usually wide, nearly flat on top, rounded on the sides, and tapered toward a narrow breast. The rump is wide and round, and curved up to a stubby undersized tail. The body sections are often held together by dowels as well as nails. These birds vary more in shape than those of the Stratford School. Pine and cedar are the common woods of construction, but a few birds are known with bodies of mahogany. The Milford decoys lacked the advantage of easy pickup by the tails which served as handles for the Stratford birds.

Old hollow Milford black duck. Similar to the style adopted by Cassius Smith. Private collection.

Typical Milford black duck; possibly by Cassius Smith. Private collection.

CASSIUS SMITH (1847-1907)

Cassius Smith, who gunned for the table of his brother's George Smith Hotel in Milford, was the best known carver in the Milford style because he identified much of his work by the brand, "C. SMITH". He was an excellent craftsman and made scaup and goldeneye decoys with a characteristic fat-bodied shape. Smith commonly weighted his decoys with an inletted rectangle of poured lead, but on some he attached the weights.

Similar but smaller scaup and old squaws with "S & S" carved in the bottom are examples of the Milford style. They were said by William Mackey to have been made about 1875 by George and Minor Smith, brothers of Milford. These are attractive little short-tailed birds, hollow-carved, and with two dowels running through the body. A good many decoys by the same maker(s) are found without brand or initials.

A group of beautifully carved and superbly painted full-bodied hollow decoys with inletted weights and a distinctly Milford form were found in eastern Long Island. They were acquired by Roy Young of Mattituck shortly after World War II, and he branded them "R. A. YOUNG". They were on display for a while in a small Museum at Mattituck, but are now dispersed. Others by the same maker have the carved initials, "E. F. H.". The earlier history of these birds is sketchy and accounts are conflicting. One account holds that they were made by a Long Island carver, and another that they were picked up on the Long Island beach, having washed over the Sound from Connecticut. The case for their Connecticut origin is strengthened by the fact that many examples of the general form by different makers are found in Connecticut, while Long Island's north shore decoys were typically crude solid blocks.

Cassius Smith hen goldeneye; paint by Shang Wheeler. Private collection.

Bottom view of Cassius Smith goldeneye. Private collection.

Some collectors have argued, because these decoys have Cassius Smith features, that he made them. Lacking another name to identify them, auction houses have attributed them to Smith, but the workmanship is better than that of any birds bearing his brand. The species with Smith's brand are limited to goldeneye and scaup, while the Long Island group contains not only these but also mallard, bufflehead, widgeon, and red-breasted merganser. If these birds were made by Cassius Smith, he was demonstrating skill not otherwise shown. The most convincing argument that they were not made by him is seen in comparison of X-ray photographs. Smith attached the head with two screws from beneath. The maker of Young's birds used two screws from above, through the forward-protruding neck section. The body sections of Smith's birds were held together by wire nails, while for Young's "elegant unknowns" six long screws were used.

Other wide-bodied decoys found on Long Island have also been assigned to Connecticut. A very old black duck from a group found on the beach near Orient, Long Island, is shown on page 132. It could be a predecessor and prototype for the Young and Cassius Smith birds. Its body is wider and flatter, and the body halves are fastened by forged nails, but the head is attached like the Youngs. The weight is a flat rectangle of lead, held on by copper nails rather than inletted.

Milford scaup. Unbranded but attributed to Cassius Smith. Private collection.

Cassius Smith goldeneye drake. No brand. Attached weights are stamped "FB". Private collection.

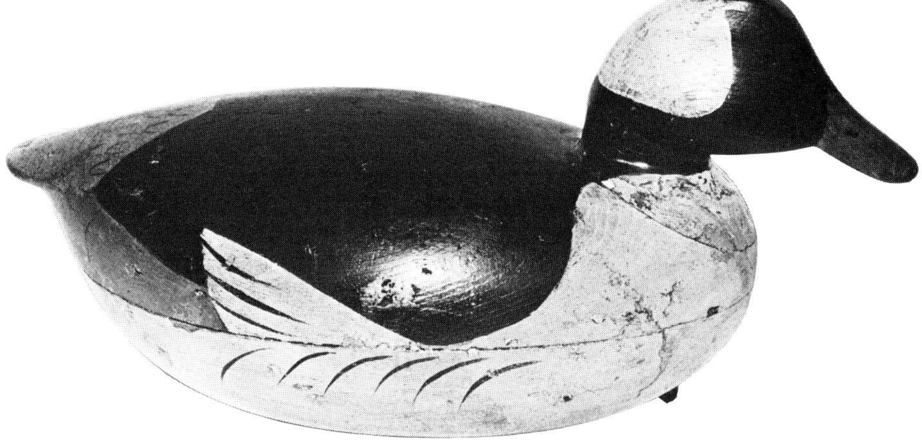

Bufflehead, Milford. "Elegant unknown" attributed by some to Cassius Smith. Private collection.

"Elegant unknown" merganser attributed with question to Cassius Smith. Private collection.

Mallard drake by same maker as the other "elegant unknowns". Private collection.

ARTHUR BALDWIN

Most of the older gunners used strings of decoys of mixed origin. An example is Arthur Baldwin, who was an active gunner in the last quarter of the nineteenth century. He is credited with having made the wide-bodied scaup carrying his "BALDWIN" brand. Though he lived in Stratford these birds are of the Milford type. Other decoys that he used and branded were produced by different makers and some are of the Stratford form, including examples by Holmes and Laing.

Arthur Baldwin scaup made c. 1880-1890. Private collection.

Bottom view of Arthur Baldwin scaup, showing "BALDWIN" brand and history written by Charles Disbrow in 1953.

Arthur Baldwin bird of c. 1890 with head replacement by Bliss c. 1910. Private collection.

Scaup by the Milford Smith brothers, with carved initials "S & S". Bill has been replaced. Private collection.

Another Milford "S & S" type bird, with original but worn bill. Private collection.

Milford unknown. Private collection.

A Milford scaup of extreme breadth. Maker unknown. Private collection.

Broadbill sleeper by an unknown Milford carver. Private collection.

Unknown Milford scaup, owned by R. I. Culver, and so branded. Private collection.

Milford scoter. Maker unknown. Shelburne Museum.

Old Milford whistler by unknown maker 1901. Owned by Les Ferris. Private collection.

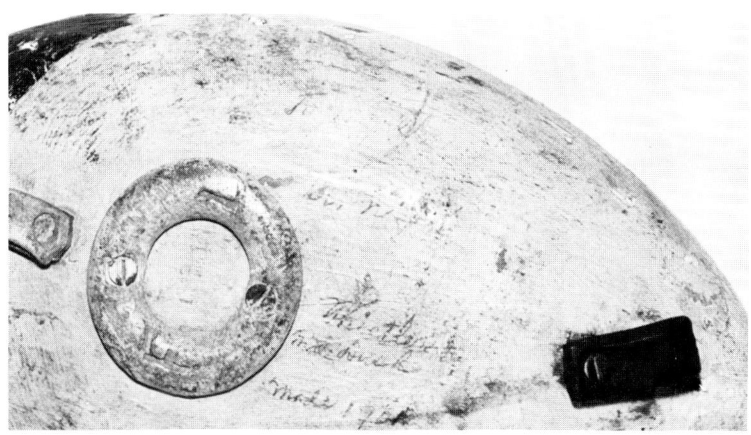

Bottom of Milford whistler. Circular weight is stamped "L. FERRIS". Written in pencil: "To my friend Dr. N. Friedman. Whistler male duck. Made 1901. L. S. Ferris". Private collection.

HOWARD HOADLEY

Decoys of the Stratford style continued to be popular and were made and used by Stratford gunners as well as by residents of the neighboring communities of Bridgeport, Southport, and Westport. The Milford style, however, lost favor and was seldom used for construction of decoys after the turn of the century. One man, Howard Hoadley of Milford, did make hollow wooden decoys in a modified Milford style in the 1920s. He also made cork-bodied decoys with wood bottom-boards in the 1930s. Hoadley's birds were generally weighted by inletted poured lead of an oval shape, but on some he used an attached elliptical or ovoid weight.

In the Housatonic region as elsewhere, there were always a few individuals who did not follow the conventions of the time and who made decoys of their own design and which cannot be classed as either "Stratford" or "Milford". Examples are Charles Disbrow's early work and the heavy-billed, multilayered birds from Milford that have been attributed (probably incorrectly) to Disbrow.

Hoadley black duck, 1920s. Private collection.

Hoadley sleeper from same rig as previous black duck. Private collection.

Hoadley cork black duck, 1930s. Private collection.

III.
The Connecticut River Region (Essex, Lyme, Old Saybrook)

The tidewater section of the Connecticut River, with its mid-seventeenth century settlements of Saybrook, Lyme, and Essex, has been a long-established gunning center. As the nineteenth century neared its end, the earlier market hunters slowly gave way to sportsmen, who hunted for pleasure. They supported professional guides and bought up the better shooting areas for private use.

The Potopaug Gun Club, situated in Lord's Cove, Lyme, was a prominent center of sporting activities. It was formed shortly after 1900 and still exists. Some of its founders, Leonard Comstock, Ben Harrison, Walter Kopke, Bill Sangster, Reginald Herring, Mort Johns, and others, are remembered by today's hunters. In the beginning, the Potopaug Gun Club members used a combination of live ducks and decoys, mostly by Sam Collins. Subsequently, they added cork decoys from various sources, and later used Wildfowler decoys.

In spite of the extensive gunning activity on the lower Connecticut River, the area produced only two outstanding decoy makers, Samuel Collins, Jr. and Ted Mulliken. Collins carved for himself and local gunners, and Mulliken founded the Wildfowler Decoy Company and produced decoys used throughout the country. Both made quality birds, Collins in large numbers from about 1875 to 1930, and Mulliken in much greater quantity from about 1920 to 1957. Mulliken entered the National Decoy Contests and won many prizes in both the professional machine-made and hand-made classes. His commercial operation is discussed under the "Factory Decoys" heading.

There were many Connecticut River gunners who made a few decoys for their own use. Most of them imitated the Collins form, but a few did not. None produced decoys of quality or in numbers sufficient to merit much recognition, but examples of their work are shown.

Positive identification of the makers of many Connecticut River decoys, as is true for other regions as well, is sometimes impossible. Decoys that emerge from attics and barns in small groups, representing the hunting rigs of predecessors of individuals living today, are found without records. The current owner may know that a father or grandfather used them and also insist that he made them, but the evidence is often unconvincing. A further difficulty with attribution is that people who consider themselves knowledgeable give positive but conflicting statements, because of a lack of complete knowledge and a compulsion to speak with authority.

For most of the decoys pictured, evidence was weighed from several sources and provenience given accordingly. "Made by" or "by" indicates a very high probability. "Attributed to" or "assigned to" indicates a probability of fifty percent or more, or the unconfirmed statement of a person whose opinion is respected.

The Connecticut River, like the Housatonic with its Albert Laing, had a man who set the distinctive local decoy pattern. His name was Samuel Collins, but there has been some uncertainty on whether he was Sam Collins, Senior or Junior. Timothy Eastland, a Connecticut River collector, cites a merganser that an earlier owner had attributed to Sam Collins, Sr., and from examination of many Collins decoys, he says he detects differences that indicate the work of at least two Collins carvers. If this view is accepted, one must conclude that Sam Collins, Sr. (or possibly an earlier unknown maker) introduced the form and that it was followed closely by his son and other makers of the region.

Positive attribution of decoys to father or son is questionable, and most of those surviving today were probably made by Sam Collins, Jr. Except for appearance suggesting greater age, which can be misleading, the general differences have to do with body thickness and head position. Sam Collins, Sr. is asserted to have made the birds with the thinner bodies, and heads held in a more relaxed attitude. According to Eastland, the distinguishing difference is in the head placement, with the juncture of the bill and head nearly even with the front of the breast for the son's birds and farther aft and with shorter necks for the father's.

Ned Pratt and Mort Johns at the Potapaug Gun Club, late 1930s. Courtesy of Don Doyle.

The establishment of Sam Collins, Sr. as a carver, based on the documentary evidence and the sculptural details noted, is tenuous. It seems possible that all of the Collins decoys were made by Sam Collins, Jr. He was an active carver for sixty years, and it would be surprising if some deviation from a fixed pattern had not occurred during this time. The thickness of body may have been imposed more by the thickness of the lumber available at the time than by precise design. The differences among Collins decoys are less pronounced than in the decoys of almost every other well-known carver. Collins birds pictured will be identified simply as by "Sam Collins" and, except in special cases noted, it is assumed that the maker was Sam Collins, Jr.

The Collinses lived in Essex, and the distinctive shape of the birds is known as the "Collins" or "Essex" form. The body is shallow and almond-shaped. The top and bottom are about equally rounded to the sides which curve to a small short tail. The head is narrow, and an extension forward from a rather thin neck provides a good base for nailing to the body. A dowel runs through the head to facilitate its attachment and strengthen the neck. Eyes are painted or lacking. Eyes of tacks or glass, that may have been added later, are found on a few birds. Ballast weights are rectangular pieces of lead, nailed on. Known species are black duck, scaup, goldeneye, bufflehead, and American merganser.

Collins bodies and heads were commonly made of solid pine. A few with hollow bodies have been found. They were hollowed in an unusual way, presumably by the owner. He split the body into an upper and lower half, hollowed out each, and then recombined the halves and nailed them together.

Essex and its environs was the only area in Connecticut known to the writer where American merganser decoys were made, and Sam Collins was the best known maker. Because of his unique method of constructing the head, his mergansers are often mistakenly thought to have been reheaded. He attached to the body a lower neck section of pine that extended forward as in his other birds, and to this he fitted and dowelled a head of oak with a thin merganser bill. Through the greater strength of oak he lessened the chances of breakage. Other American mergansers from the region have one-piece short-necked heads of pine, with pattern otherwise like Collins'. Sam Collins, Sr. may have been the maker of some of them.

Collins' birds have a characteristic but not very realistic shape. The bodies are too thin and the heads are generally undersized and too narrow. The bills of scaup are not wide enough to deserve the common

American merganser by Sam Collins of Essex. Private collection.

American merganser by Sam Collins. Shelburne Museum.

Collins American merganser—Head and neck of one piece. Attributed to Sam Collins, Sr. Branded "E.B. WKS". Swanson collection.

name for the species, "broadbill". The only differences between broadbill and black ducks were in size and painting. In spite of the artist's license for departure from nature, and whatever the critical appraisal by a live duck might be, the form of a true Collins is pleasing to the eye of the collector.

Collins decoys, like Masons and others with solid body and no keel, rolled in an unducklike manner in the water. When Wildfowlers, with their stabilizing keels became available, most Connecticut River hunters switched to them.

Connecticut River decoys are largely intact, each one the work of an individual, as contrasted with Stratford and Milford decoys, so many of which have been reheaded or given other repairs necessitated from the damage by salt water where they were used.

A listing of the recognized regional makers, with biographical notes and description of their decoys, based on available information, follows:

Collins black duck attributed to Samuel Collins, Sr.
Private collection.

Sam Collins black duck. Private collection.

Scaup drake by Sam Collins of Essex. Private collection.

SAMUEL COLLINS, SR.

Very little is known about Sam Collins, Sr. He was an Essex boat builder and a sea captain, born probably c. 1830. He is thought to have died at sea. Besides his namesake, he had at least one other son, Deacon, who also made decoys, reputedly similar to those of Samuel, Jr.

SAMUEL COLLINS, JR. (1854-1948)

Sam Collins, Jr., because of his long life of 94 years, was well known to several generations of Essex residents. He was a master of all trades—an oysterman, a carpenter, and a builder of schooners and smaller boats. He was highly regarded by hunters for his shallow-draft sculling boats and rail boats. He also captained sailing vessels that carried freight between Connecticut and Long Island.

Duck hunting was a pursuit of his youth that he gave up with advancing age, but he continued to push for rail hunters when in his eighties. He made black duck, scaup, goldeneye, bufflehead, and American merganser decoys for many years and found ready sale for them to local sportsmen, notably of the Potopaug Gun Club of Lord's Cove, in Lyme. He is remembered as an old bachelor and completely bald.

Essex contemporaries and younger neighbors of Sam Collins copied his style but never quite equalled his artistry.

Hollow-carved scaup attributed to Sam Collins. Note height of seam on right side compared with height on companion photo of left side. Private collection.

Left side of previous bird. The splitting and hollowing may have been done by its owner, and not by Collins.

Sam Collins scaup duck. Private collection.

Sam Collins goldeneye drake. Private collection.

This hen scaup is attributed to Deacon Collins, Samuel's brother. Private collection.

Pair of American mergansers made by Franklin W. Adams of Essex. Private collection.

Pair of scaup decoys from the gunning rig of Reginald I. Herring of Essex. Made by Frank Adams. Private collection.

American merganser drake by an unknown Essex maker. The Collins influence is apparent. Private collection.

Black duck by Herb Banning of Essex. Private collection.

Goldeneye attributed to Bill Webber of Essex. Private collection.

Black duck by Ned Pratt of Essex. Private collection.

Black duck attributed to Sam Hunt of Essex. Private collection.

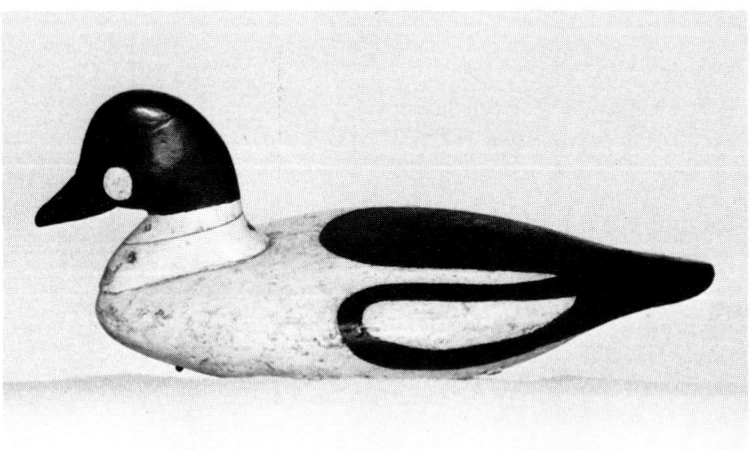

A fine goldeneye from Essex. Head and neck made in two pieces. Branded and attributed to "G. B. HAYDEN." Private collection.

NED PRATT (c. 1885-1970)

Pratt was a member of an old Essex family and lived there all his life. He was a waterman and a market gunner for ducks and rail. He made decoys, (black ducks only known) with deeper bodies than Collins. They were hollow and held together by two dowels and nails. Heads were attached by dowels and fitted with tack eyes. The juncture of the head and neck was deeply cut, almost suggesting a chin.

HERBERT BANNING (-c. 1960)

Herbert Banning of Hamburg Cove was a cabinet maker and boat builder. He made black duck decoys in the 1920s. They resemble Collins' in outline but the heads are larger and held more stiffly erect, and have tack eyes. The bottoms are flat, and the decoy pictured has a diamond-shaped lead weight attached by four brass screws.

FRANKLIN W. ADAMS (c. 1902-)

Frank Adams moved from Maine to Essex in 1922 at age 20. The decoys, scaup and black ducks, that have been attributed to him appear stiff-necked and have flat bottoms, fitted with bar-type lead weights with pointed ends. Following the Maine tradition, he inletted the heads into the body, in contrast to Collins who attached them flat.

His son, Frank W. Adams, Jr. made almost identical decoys, but with heads not inletted.

WILLIAM WEBBER (-c. 1969)

Bill Webber was an Essex fisherman and hunter. His decoys, apparently only black ducks, though with a Collins look, are chunkier and the neck extension is less pronounced. The decoy pictured has an inletted round weight and screw-eyes in the bottom fore and aft for use in a continuous rig.

SAM HUNT (-c. 1950)

Sam Hunt of Essex followed the Collins pattern fairly closely, except that his birds (blacks and scaup) had a racy look, with pointed high-raised breasts. The heads were rounded, with a chin-like protrusion downward at the base of the bill.

JUDY PHELPS (-1952)

Judy Phelps was an active carver of Essex in the 1920s and later. He made black duck decoys that look like Collinses but are hollow, and he inletted the lead weights. He also carved shore birds, but only after shore bird shooting became illegal. These must be classed as decoratives.

BERTRAM TOOKER

Bertram Tooker was a partner of Sam Collins, Jr. in some of his endeavors, but in vocation he was an employee of a local Witch Hazel manufacturing plant. He was a gunner who made unimpressive solid pine scaup decoys for his own use. Unfortunately, he was not influenced by his association with Collins to the extent of copying is style.

JAMES G. HURLBURT

The best looking decoy from the Connecticut River region known to the writer was a goldeneye inscribed "Howard Gladding, from Coit Gladding Estate 1918. . Made by James G. Hurlburt". It was a lifelike individual creation, showing no trace of Collins' influence. The body was full and perfectly shaped, and the detail of bill carving especially noteworthy.

OLIVER LA PLACE (b. 1901)

Oliver La Place, a highly respected hunting guide for over fifty years, is almost a legend on the Connecticut River. Born in Lyme in 1901, he moved to Essex ten years later and has lived there ever since. The outdoors is his love and guiding was his favorite professional occupation. During the off-season he was a boat builder. He retired from this activity in 1969, and now traps muskrats, raccoons, foxes, and snapping turtles for income.

La Place began hunting black ducks with live mallard decoys, but since live decoys were not available for broadbill, goldeneyes, and mergansers, he started making wooden ones in the early 20s, and when live decoys were outlawed, he replaced them all by wood and cork substitutes. He estimates his total production at more than one hundred of wood and four hundred of cork. One winter he made a pair of every kind of duck shot in the area—twelve in all, plus a pair of Canada geese. They were put on display by Chris Percy of the Connecticut River Watershed Council. La Place's wife, Mary, whom he married in 1925, did most of his painting. He has made other decoratives, eiders, shore birds, and an owl, and is still carving.

Oliver La Place knew Sam Collins and was given a merganser by Collins as a wedding present. He did not copy Collins but made decoys in his own style, somewhat crude, as though the details in finishing the carving had been neglected. He did not quite capture the look of real life or of folk art.

SWEDE LARSON

A contemporary of Oliver La Place, and also a hunting guide, was "Swede" Larson of Saybrook. Like La Place, he hunted rail in the marshes off Essex. He also hunted ducks, using crude, boxy cork decoys that he made. After a hunt, he frequently sold some of them to his clients at $1.50 each. One wonders how he managed to get so high a price for these "ugly ducklings."

Oliver La Place at 80, holding recently built broadbills. In the background are some of his earlier gunning black ducks—cork with Wildfowler heads.

Oliver La Place broadbill pair, of his own collection.

Pair of mallards by La Place. His own collection.

Swede Larson gunning decoy. Private collection.

Hen scaup used and possibly made by the Smith family of East Haddam, Connecticut. Private collection.

Scaup duck, Smith family of East Haddam. Repainted by Marion Harris of Old Saybrook. Private collection.

HARRY ROSS (b. 1914)

Harry Ross had an important position as designer with the Wildfowler Company. Mulliken's success in the decoy carving contests spurred Ross to also enter the competition. He won a good many ribbons and in a few classes gained the edge over Mulliken, who, it was said, resented being outdone by an employee. Ross resigned from Wildfowler and enlisted in the Navy during World War II. He is now retired and lives in Higganum, Connecticut.

Harry Ross should be credited for much of the design of Wildfowler working decoys, but those that he made by his own hand were intended for competition and display, and not actual use. These birds reflect a "super" Wildfowler look in both carving and painting.

THE HARRISES

The Harris couple, Richard (1910-1980) and Marion (b. 1914) were both long-time employees of Wildfowler. He did the finishing work on decoys and she was chief painter. Richard Harris continued to make decoys on his own after the factory burned in 1957, until he died in 1980. Harris followed the Wildfowler pattern but put more emphasis on finish and paint. Most of his carvings were made without keels and are better classified as decorative objects than as decoys.

LESSER KNOWN AND CONTEMPORARY CARVERS

Other names of the general area associated with decoys were Rob Miller, Joe DeWolfe, Philip C. Fairbanks, senior and junior, Allen Carlson along with several other Carlsons, and the Bushnells. The David Bushnell family of Westbrook used, and possibly made, decoys with full bodies and inletted heads. A decoy by an unknown maker from Deep River, above Essex, has the Collins form.

The lower Connecticut River region has produced several professional artists, David Ward, Timothy Eastland, Mark McNair, and Chet Reneson, who have capitalized on the recent popularity of bird carvings. All have made some excellent decoys, but their main goal, with the exception of Reneson, has been to attract customers, not wildfowl.

Moving up the Connecticut River beyond the tide into fresh and swifter water, the number of ducks and gunners diminishes. Hunters plied the wide and shallow waters around Hadlyme and Haddam Meadows, and others were active upriver at Glastonbury. Some who made decoys were Frank Banning of Hadlyme, Aaron Hall of Haddam Meadows, and Wesley Gordeaux of Glastonbury. There were undoubtedly others unknown.

Goldeneye made by James G. Hurlburt probably pre-1900. Private collection.

IV.
The Middle Coastal Region (New Haven, Branford, Guilford)

The meandering coastline between the Housatonic and Connecticut rivers is filled with coves and small bays that are ideal feeding grounds for waterfowl. Branford, with its inlets and offshore cluster of small islands, the Thimbles, has been known for generations as a favorite center for duck hunting.

The history of gunning in the area is not well documented, and information of the gunners and decoy makers before 1920 is very sketchy. Shang Wheeler in his chapter in Connet's *Duck Shooting Along the Atlantic Tidewater* spins yarns about the long-range shooting of "Hen" Murray (1870-1933) and Dr. Charles Porter (1871-1951) of Branford. These men, along with Eugene Shepherd and Charles Lanfare, were early contemporaries with whom he hunted. There is no evidence that any of them made decoys.

Most areas with good duck shooting seemed to develop a local style of decoy, and Branford was no exception. The typical hand-carved "Branford" decoys are generally chunky and heavy. They were weighted with lead, inletted or attached in the form of lumps, cut sheet, or cast in the shape of a long shallow keel. The outstanding characteristic of Branford decoys is found in the carving of the head, which commonly has fat cheeks or jowls. The heads are reminiscent of Ira Hudson of Chincoteague, Virginia, and are inletted into the body in the manner of some Maine decoys.

The Shelburne Museum catalog shows a white-winged scoter said to have been made before the Civil War by Ralph Lamphere of Branford. It is high-necked, and though cruder and not much like the later Branford style in most respects, it does seem to have their typical fat cheeks. The names Lamphere and Lanfare are probably variations or misspellings of Lanphier, one of the early families who settled in Branford.

The originator of the Branford style is unknown, and assignment of Branford decoys to specific makers is difficult. Many of them seemed to have followed the general pattern common to the region. "Flip" Goodsell of Stratford used decoys that his son Fred said were made by a cousin, William Stannard (1874-1931) of Branford. In the Goodsell rig are a few of poorer and some of better workmanship, possibly made by other members of the family. Some of the best have arched tails and have been attributed to Charles Haines, a Branford cabinet maker. Other makers credited with Branford style work are William Flanders, George Mason, John Kells, Rudy Illig (1865-1952), Otto Illig (1906-1971), and Frank Harlow. Several of the Shelburne Museum's collection of Branford decoys were sold at the Richard A. Bourne auction in 1985. One was made about 1904 by Robert S. Bradley (1874-1969), and two were attributed to William Stannard.

Broadbills make up about ninety percent of the decoys found around Branford, the remainder being black ducks, scoters, and old squaws. Some of the Branford gunners made cork black ducks of little artistic merit, and a few also made cork scoters. Merganser decoys from the area are not known to the writer.

The reason for the preponderance of broadbill decoys is that the species of both lesser and greater scaup were the prime quarry, and they are still abundant. Because of the limited extent of marshland, black ducks have always been less numerous. Some individuals hunted black ducks, but with broadbills offering a much better prospect for a successful hunt, professional guides and nearly all private hunters concentrated on them.

CLIFFORD COLLINS

Louis Uhl, a Branford hunter, fisherman, and lobsterman, now in his 70s, introduced the writer to a colorful old-timer, Cliff Collins, who has been known for many years as an outstanding authority on duck hunting. He enjoyed telling us that he was "sixteen—eight and eight". Then eighty-eight, he is now in his 90s. Cliff made his living on the water, mostly from lobstering. He also "winkled" the oyster beds for pay by the oyster growers, using 310 periwinkle pots baited with horseshoe crabs. He was paid two dollars a bushel for the periwinkles; a record catch was 59 bushels. He had interesting stories of the great hunting of earlier days off Branford when there was no season, no limit, and no license. He loaded his own shells for years but later bought factory rejects for a penny apiece. Cliff Collins made for his own use cork decoys that resembled those from the Tux-Dux factory. Among the other decoys he used were some attractive-looking undersized wood old squaws that he got from Jim Carden. He also used chunky wood decoys that he got from, and were probably made by, J. Ray MacClain. They were of two-piece construction and had inletted rectangular lead weights.

FRANK HARLOW (1873-1968)

Frank Harlow was a stone mason by trade but spent a lot of time on the water—lobstering, fishing, clamming, oystering, and duck hunting. He was well-known as a local character in Branford, living to the age of 95. He was easily identified at a distance on the water by his method of rowing a boat in the "backwater" position. When questioned about the backward rowing, his reply was always that he knew where he had been but wanted to know where he was going.

Harlow made duck decoys—in large number, according to his daughter, but none are now identified. His ability as a craftsman was demonstrated in his yellowlegs shore bird decoys. They were well-styled working birds, painted with muted and blended colors.

Usually a lone hunter, Frank Harlow occasionally took along one or two of his daughters for company.

PROFESSIONAL GUIDES

In the 1920s and up until World War II there were more professional guides along this section of the coast than anywhere else in Connecticut. Lonny Ganung of West Haven, Steve Thomas and Charles Bartlett of East Haven, Cliff Collins and the Bradley brothers of Branford, and Joe Dolan of Guilford took out parties of sportsmen who came from New York and the cities of New Jersey and Connecticut.

Factory decoys, Mason, Pratt, and Dodge, and later, Wildfowler and Tux-Dux were favored by the professional guides, but most of them used mixed rigs, a motley collection of factory and hand-made birds. Exceptions to the rule were Steve Thomas and Lonny Ganung, who made and used credible decoys.

SERENO STEPHEN THOMAS (1865-1938)

Steve Thomas, of East Haven, was one of the early professional guides. He made decoys for his own use and for sale. He left a ledger dated 1909-1910, in which he showed patterns for ducks and a yellowlegs. The yellowlegs was well proportioned, but to the writer's knowledge, no Steve Thomas shore birds have been identified. His ledger showed delivery of 40 broadbills, 8 whistlers, and 20 anchors on January 28, 1910, and on January 30, 6 black ducks, 8 whistlers, 31 old squaws, 13 coot, and 40 broadbills. Patterns for mallard drake and hen are pictured.

Of the Steve Thomas birds examined, broadbills were made of solid pine, some with carved outlines of wings, and his black ducks were of two-piece hollow construction, with carved wings, raised to a joined single tip. All were well formed and had carved eyes. Weights were rectangles of sheet lead or round, hammered lumps.

Steve Thomas' favorite time for hunting was at night under a full moon, and his favorite spots were the Quinnipiac Marshes and Savon Rock Marsh.

LON GANUNG (1883-1972)

Lon or Lonny Ganung, of West Haven, was a close associate of Steve Thomas, and also a professional guide.

Ganung decoys, mallard and black duck, have a plump appearance and are hollow, usually made in three layers, and have carved wings with the tips raised. This style, formerly credited to Ganung, now appears to have originated with his older friend and mentor, Steve Thomas. The Ganung birds are better known because more of them still exist in good condition. Most of the Thomas birds remaining have suffered damage from age and neglect.

CHARLES ROBERT BARTLETT (1892-1953)

Charles Bartlett of East Haven was a professional guide who took out gunning parties in the 1920s and 30s. He made a few nondescript black duck decoys with factory-turned heads, but most of his rig was made up of factory birds—Mason, Dodge, and Victor. All were deeply branded with his name and address.

JOSEPH S. DOLAN (b. 1905)

Joe Dolan of Guilford began guiding hunting parties while still in his teens. He worked the waters from New Haven to the Connecticut River for twenty-five years, the last twenty with his brother Frank, or "Nook."

Joe Dolan grew up to become a successful banker, but maintained his interest in sporting activities, especially duck hunting. He used commercial decoys and those made by his father, but never made any himself. His father and his uncle, John, were hunters and both made plain crudely fashioned decoys. His father also made a set of tin silhouette yellowlegs that he used for hunting on the beaches of Rhode Island.

TODAY'S GUNNERS

Edward Gessner of Branford hunts with eighty-year-old decoys made by his wife's grandfather, R. S. Bradley. His rig also contains birds of his own make. There are two different styles. One resembles the Bradley decoys and the other is copied from Joel Barber. Oliver "Bud" Beckley and his younger friend, Grant Briggs, hunt with a mixed rig of battered decoys, largely factory birds, that include a few old Branford broadbills. Cliff Collins' son, Fred, hunts regularly with Tux-Dux decoys and Louis Uhl used Wildfowlers.

Branford scaup by an unknown maker. Private collection.

Scaup by William Stannard of Branford. From the rig of his cousin, "Flip" Goodsell of Stratford. Private collection.

Scoop-tailed scaup attributed to Charles Haines of Branford.

Branford scaup. Attributed to R. S. Bradley, 1904. Shelburne Museum.

Old squaw by Jim Carden of Branford. Private collection.

Black duck made by Steve Thomas. Private collection.

Steve Thomas scaup with carved wings. Private collection.

Lon Ganung of West Haven. Hen mallard or black duck. Private collection.

Ganung black duck with turned head. Bourne Auction.

V.
The Eastern End of the Connecticut Coast (Mystic, Stonington, Noank)

The kinds and numbers of migrating water birds found in any location depend upon its environment and its position relative to major flyways. Connecticut and Rhode Island have coastlines of widely different character, and distinct bird populations. The coast of Rhode Island from Point Judith to Watch Hill is fairly straight, with beaches that are attractive to shore birds, but with few bays or inlets to attract ducks. By contrast, The Connecticut coast, from the entrance to Stonington Harbor westward, is very irregular, with lots of inlets where ducks can feed and rest. Consequently, Rhode Island has been a haven for shore birds and Connecticut a preferred stopover for migrating waterfowl. This situation has produced an overlap of hunters from one state to the other. Connecticut gunners have habitually gone to Rhode Island to shoot shore birds and Rhode Islanders have come to Connecticut for ducks.

The two main streams of ducks migrating through Connecticut in the fall, as mentioned earlier, come down the coast and down the Connecticut River. Where the two streams join at the mouth of the Connecticut River, some flocks fan out eastward temporarily but most continue southwestwardly down the coast or fly across the Sound to Long Island. The western portion of the Connecticut coast benefits from both sources, while the eastern end receives few of the Connecticut River migrants and is thus limited in the numbers of ducks, especially puddlers, that move through. Here the duck population is made up chiefly of deep divers. In this area shelldrakes or red-breasted mergansers were hunted extensively and it is here that one finds the highest concentration of merganser decoys.

The early settlers of the region made their living from the sea as sealers, whalers, and fishermen. Some were also hunters of waterfowl, not for sport but for food, and most apparently hunted without decoys. Those who used decoys made their own and none exhibited much artistic talent. The species most commonly seen are the shelldrake, bufflehead, broadbill, and goldeneye, all made with solid pine bodies. The workmanship is usually crude.

Stick-up silhouette brant from Nathaniel Palmer rig. Private collection.

NATHANIEL B. PALMER (1799-1877)

The earliest Connecticut hunter of ducks and shore birds of whom we have any knowledge was Nathaniel B. Palmer, of Stonington. He was a sportsman, a ship's captain, and an important entrepreneur of his day.

Palmer assumed the responsibilities of an adult very early in life, sailing on a blockade runner in the War of 1812. He joined the sealing fleet while in his teens and quickly advanced in position. He became captain of the sloop *Hero* and, in 1821 at the age of twenty-two, attained fame as discoverer of the Antarctic Continent. Palmerland and the Palmer Archipelago are name for him.

Palmer operated his business from New York and Stonington. Among his accomplishments were the designing, building, and commanding the clipper ship *Houqua* that in 1844 set the record time for sailing from New York to Hong Kong.

Palmer hunted waterfowl and shore birds in Connecticut and Rhode Island. Having no children to inherit his possessions, he left his decoys to a hunting companion who passed them down through several generations of his own descendants, one of whom gave a major portion of the group to the Old Lighthouse Museum in Stonington. The full-bodied yellowlegs and knots appear to be the oldest. The duck decoys, as well as the silhouettes of brant and greater yellowlegs, could possibly be later additions to the original lot. It is presumed, but not proven, that Captain Nathaniel Palmer made the decoys he used.

MOSES H. WILCOX (1858-1963)

A most colorful early duck hunter was Moses Wilcox of Quiambaug and of Mystic. He was from a family of seafaring tradition that goes back 300 years to Edmund Wilcox, who joined Roger Williams in the founding of Rhode Island.

Moses Wilcox started commercial fishing at the age of 16, and at 21 had a steamboat pilot's license. He sailed the Atlantic coast between Mystic and North Carolina with the menhaden fleet. He lived an active life for 105 years. The New London Day newspaper, in an article commemorating his one hundred and fifth birthday, stated that "Captain Moses H. Wilcox of Quiambaug is the only man who ever had a sperm whale by the tail." This happened in the late 1800s in Fisher's Island Sound. Wilcox lassoed the whale from a dory and towed it ashore and beached it.

Wilcox made and hunted with decoys. Some, mergansers especially, were of the conventional form, solid wood and painted. But for black ducks, he covered the blocks with duck skins to achieve a more natural looking, completely feathered body.

Merganser from Mystic. Maker Moses Wilcox. Private collection.

Merganser by Moses Wilcox of Mystic. Private collection.

JAMES HALSTEAD BROWN (1890-1974)

James Halstead Brown, known as Halstead, seems to have been the only twentieth century decoy maker of the region worthy of the classification of craftsman, though some of his predecessors were commendable. His many mergansers, broadbills, and buffleheads are better looking than any turned out by his contemporaries. He was painstaking in his work, and mounted the head on a raised partial neck extension of the body.

Halstead Brown was a life-long resident of Noank. He was a painter by profession but held several different positions with the government of the village of Noank, including Fire Chief. He was an outdoorsman, a Boy Scout leader, a collector of stamps, coins, and Indian artifacts, and a whittler. In addition to the decoys, for which he is best known, he whittled a large number of canes from unusual saplings he found on his walks through the woods.

LOUIS BAYER (b. 1906)

Louis Bayer was a game warden for the State of Connecticut for 32 years, and it was he who supplied much of the information on duck population and gunning in the area.

Lou Bayer was born in New York City but grew up on a farm in North Ashford, Connecticut. He moved to Niantic in 1926. He was a hunter and hunting guide before becoming a game warden. He was associated with the State's program of raising and stocking mallards, in the 1940s; before that time they were almost unknown in Connecticut.

Bayer made 30 or 40 broadbills, a dozen buffleheads, a few whistlers, and about 50 black ducks. All were made of wood, except the black ducks, which were of cork composite with one-inch wood bottoms. He also made black duck "kidders", as he called them, rump or tail sections weighted to simulate ducks feeding with their heads submerged. On these he nailed legs cut from red inner-tube rubber.

Early acquaintances of Bayer who also made decoys were Captain George Smith and Frank Banning, as well as Halstead Brown, previously mentioned. Some of the later and current gunners include Duke Dudkowski, Fred Ewalt, the Sterry Brothers, and George Parker.

Hen merganser by Halstead Brown of Noank. Private collection.

Broadbill by Halstead Brown of Noank. Private collection.

Bufflehead by Halstead Brown. Private collection.

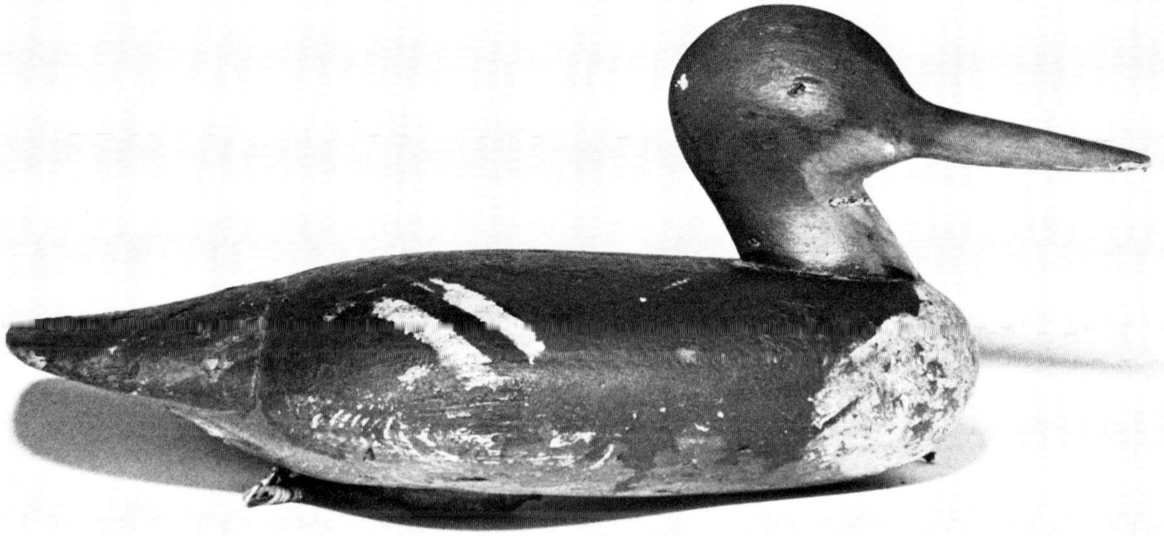

Frank Banning red-breasted merganser. Private collection.

Goldeneye drake by unknown maker from the Mystic area. Private collection.

Pair of goldeneyes from the Mystic area. Maker unknown. Private collection.

Lou Bayer black duck from his own rig.

Black ducks made by Lou Bayer. Bodies are cork with Wildfowler heads. The maker's rig.

VI. The Western End of the Connecticut Coast (Wilton, Westport, Norwalk)

The western end of Connecticut's shore between Fairfield and the New York border produced no outstanding early decoy carvers. Important residents of the area were Joel Barber of Wilton and Ralf Coykendall of Weston. Barber, through his collecting, carving, and authoritative research and writing kindled the interest in decoy collecting. Coykendall was a sportswriter and a commercial maker of decoys. His definitive book *Duck Decoys and How to Rig Them,* was published in 1955. A discussion of his commercial venture is to be found under "Factory Decoys."

Saugatuck Harbor, at the mouth of the Saugatuck River, and the neighboring waters bordering Westport, South Norwalk, and the Norwalk Islands, provided good duck hunting for the local residents, but there was no marshland like Knell's Island or extensive shallows to attract great numbers of ducks or hunters from other locations. Although a few of the local gunners made their own decoys—Leroy McElwee of Westport made 14 credible black ducks in 1945 from Wheeler patterns—no really noteworthy maker has been discovered.

Some of the contemporary gunners of this general area have made a few decoys for their personal use but most of them now rely entirely on moulded birds. Kenneth Gleason, of Darien, a carver of decoratives, made a most unusual group of decoys, 104 puffins to attract their kind, not for shooting but as part of a successful project to reestablish a nesting colony on Eastern Eggrock Island, Maine.

The Stamford-Greenwich waters around Stamford Harbor, Great Captain's Island, and the mouth of the Byram River were formerly popular gunning areas, but most of the decoys used were from out of state. One man who did make his own decoys was Michael Varady, a native of Hungary who moved to Byram and hunted there during the 1930s and 40s. Most of his decoys were crudely made from several layers of wood nailed together. One exception was an old squaw with some artistic appeal, carved from a single piece of wood, with an attached branch-type head.

An important gunning rig used by the Smith family of Byram about 1890 consisted of Dodge factory broadbills and scoters and fine New Jersey decoys, black ducks and broadbills by Joe King and mergansers and old squaws by Harry Shourds, but with not a bird of Connecticut origin in the lot.

Black duck by Joel Barber. Shelburne Museum.

JOEL BARBER (1876-1952)

Joel Barber may seem to be an intruder in a book on Connecticut decoys, since he lived only his final years, less than three, in the State. Before he became a resident, his love for decoys brought him into close contact with several notable Connecticut men with similar interests. Through his writing and drawings, Barber gave prominent recognition to Connecticut decoys. As an accepted authority on decoys, he influenced the style of several lines of commercial decoys produced in the State.

Joel Barber was born in Syracuse, New York, in 1876 and spent most of his life in his native state, chiefly as a commuter from Babylon on Long Island to New York City, with a few years of residence in Rochester and Manhattan. He moved his family to Wilton, Connecticut, in 1949.

Barber was an architect by profession. He had no interest in hunting live ducks but was possessed with a keen attraction to pursuit of their man-made imitations. He was one of the first to admire their artistry and to share this appreciation in writing. His *Wild Fowl Decoys,* the first full-length book on the subject, was published in 1934.

Barber began collecting decoys in 1919 and by 1930 had amassed the finest collection of the time. He was a friend of Shang Wheeler, and together they planned a joint exhibition of old and new decoys. A showing was sponsored by Abercrombie and Fitch in 1932. It comprised 116 of Barber's old decoys with 49 of Wheeler's new exhibition birds and five of his "rough" and ready" cork working birds.

In the mid-thirties, Barber and Ralf Coykendall decided to manufacture decoys for sale. Only a small number were made and the business, "Barber Decoys," never got off the ground. However, their efforts contributed to the style of two later, more successful, commercial operations, Ralf Coykendall's American Decoys and Ted Mulliken's Wildfowlers. The American Decoys followed the patterns set by Barber and Coykendall in the earlier Barber Decoys venture, and Barber assisted Mulliken in designing the patterns for Wildfowlers.

In 1946, Barber was approached by C. M. Woolworth, President of Animal Trap Company, to design wide-bodied decoys that were to be molded and identified with Barber's name. He apparently did not comply.

Barber's own decoys can be regarded as stylized works of art, following classical lines, as might be expected from an architect. They seem to flaunt their excellence of sculptural form and miss the natural appearance achieved by other makers. The similarity to Barber's form can be seen in the photographs of examples of American Decoys and Wildfowlers, but both of these companies, especially the latter, overcame the woody look of the Barber decoys.

Barber canvasback. Shelburne Museum.

Barber redhead. Shelburne Museum.

Joel Barber scaup with angular head and round back. Shelburne Museum.

Joel Barber scaup with round head and different body form. Shelburne Museum.

Black duck made by Leroy McElwee of Westport in 1945 from pattern furnished by Wheeler. Private collection.

Old squaw made and used by Michael Varady of Byram (Greenwich). Private collection.

VII. Factory Decoys

Only a few hunters today use hand-crafted decoys. For many years, factory birds have outnumbered the hand-carved ones floating on Connecticut waters. The Mason, Dodge, Herter, and Wildfowler companies have been well-represented. More recently, other manufacturers employing cork as well as paper-mache, rubber, and especially plastic, have attained a dominant position. As always, the primary function of the decoy has been to attract ducks but, in earlier days, it often served a secondary important function—that of providing satisfaction and pride to the owner because of its quality and beauty. Today's plastic examples are realistic and effective for their primary purpose but afford no aesthetic pleasure. They are more impressive to ducks than to man.

In addition to the host of carvers who made decoys for their own use, Connecticut also had a few commercial operations. Ben Holmes made decoys for sale only; he was not a hunter. Roswell Bliss, though a hunter who got started making his own decoys, became primarily a manufacturer for the trade. Reginald Culver made and sold decoys, but on a much smaller scale than Bliss.

EDWARD H. MULLIKEN (1896-1964) AND THE WILDFOWLER DECOY COMPANY

The man directly responsible for the largest number of decoys produced in Connecticut was Edward H. (Ted) Mulliken of Essex and later of Old Saybrook. His early occupation was raising game birds, but he was also a duck hunter. A natural extension of these interests led him to making decoys, at first for his own use and later as a business. Joel Barber, of Wilton, collaborated with Mulliken in the design of decoys for his first manufacturing venture, the Dauntless Decoy Company, of Essex. Cork-bodied geese and a few ducks were hand-made and sold under the Dauntless name.

It soon became apparent to Mulliken that profit would demand fast production and volume sales. He invested in a shoe-last lathe and went wholeheartedly into production with a newly-named company, Wildfowler Decoys, Inc., at Old Saybrook, Connecticut. The Wildfowler Company was founded by Ted Mulliken. His wife, Carmen, was the company's secretary-treasurer. Operation started in 1939 but was interrupted in 1941 when full-time work began on a U.S. Government contract to produce gunstocks for the Thompson machine gun and Garand rifle.

Decoy production was resumed as soon as the war was over, and Wildfowler became the Country's largest supplier for the post-war market, as a surge in interest in duck hunting occurred. Output of up to 15,000 in a season continued until 1957, when the factory was destroyed by fire.

Wildfowlers bear no resemblance to Collins or other Connecticut River birds. Their shape is distinctive. The back and sides are rounded gracefully to a flat bottom. For stability, all Wildfowlers were made with a keel, to which was attached a lead strip or a keel-type weight, made by the R. W. Sanford Company of Bridgeport.

The first Wildfowler decoys were made of pine, hollowed from the bottom, and fitted with an inletted bottom board. This design was soon modified by replacement of the inletted bottom board with a full-sized board that completely covered the bottom. Balsa became available after the war and it was used as the material of choice for body construction. Heads were turned from birch wood.

Wildfowlers were made for nearly all common waterfowl species and in several grades of hollow pine and balsa. They were sold in sporting goods stores in this country and some were shipped abroad. The company also sold duck heads to people who wanted to make their own decoys. This explains the reason that so many cork decoys and others with odd-shaped bodies are found with heads that look like Wildfowlers.

For large scale production of gun stocks and decoys, Mulliken was dependent upon the Wysowski Woodcarving Company, which moved from New York to Westbrook, Connecticut to accommodate the business. The Wysowskis, Joseph and his nephew, Leo, operated the company that carved the gun stocks to be finished by Mulliken, and after the war continued the collaboration with decoys. The blanks were prepared by Wildfowler, the lathe carving was done by Wysowski, using Mulliken's patterns, and the rough-carved birds were returned to Wildfowler for sanding, finishing, and painting.

The Wysowski Company also ran a small custom business of replicating decoys and decoy heads for individuals. The Laing copies that Tom Marshall and Jack Tierney hunted over were turned out by Wysowski from patterns made by Willard Baldwin, of Stratford.

Canada goose by Ted Mulliken's Dauntless Decoy Company. Cork body. Shelburne Museum.

Wildfowler Old Saybrook brand.

Pair of Wildfowler broadbills, balsa. Old Saybrook. Private collection.

Wildfowler balsa black duck. Old Saybrook. Private collection.

Regular and oversize Wildfowler balsa black ducks. Private collection.

Wildfowler mallard duck. Private collection.

Wildfowler canvasback. Hollow pine, midseam construction. Bourne auction.

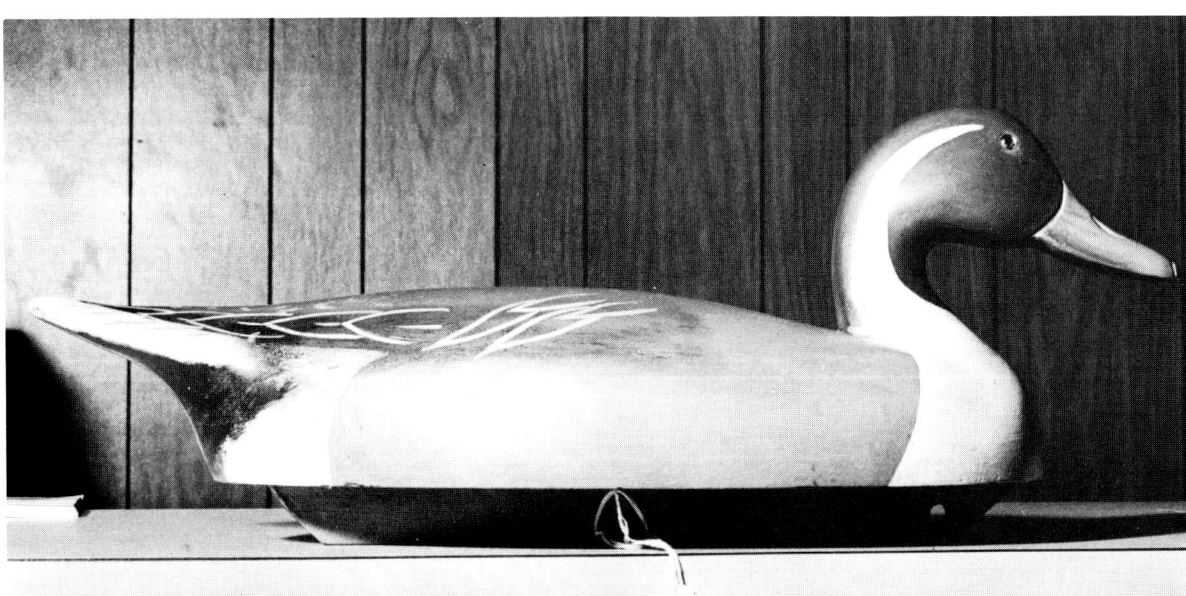

Wildfowler balsa pintail drake. Bourne auction.

Wildfowler white-winged scoter used by Louis Uhl. Hollow pine. Private collection.

Wildfowler hollow pine surf scoter from the rig of Louis Uhl. Private collection.

Wildfowler balsa eider. Private collection.

Mulliken hen bufflehead. Shelburne Museum.

Mulliken competition grade black duck. Private collection.

Ted Mulliken black duck. Fancy grade with carved wings. Private collection.

Mulliken ruddy duck. Shelburne Museum.

Fancy grade Ted Mulliken goose. Private collection.

RALF COYKENDALL AND THE NORTH AMERICAN DECOY COMPANY

Ralf Coykendall, Sr. (1892-1968) of Weston, Connecticut was a sportsman, conservationist, author, and decoy maker. Professionally, he was an advertising man with various publications, including *Cue* magazine, where he held the office of vice president and advertising manager. He was closely associated with Shang Wheeler and Joel Barber, and assisted Tom Marshall as a judge at the National Decoy Shows.

Coykendall's hand-made decoys show a strong Wheeler influence. They were carefully finished and painted and most were of exhibition quality. He first became interested in making decoys for sale in the 1930s when he and Joel Barber started—and quickly stopped—the unsuccessful venture, Barber Decoys. He made another try at commercial manufacture with his son, Ralf W. Coykendall, Jr. in the 1950s, founding the North American Decoy Company. The decoys were oversize, sturdily constructed from balsa, and fitted with hardwood heads and keels. They were sold in what Coykendall termed "natural" groups of eight—five drakes and three hens—with five different head positions, high, low, turned right, turned left, and sleeping. Depending on species they sold for $52 to $56 per set. Also available were oversize cork black ducks at $60 for a set of eight.

The North American Decoy Company remained in business only four or five years, being unable to compete successfully with the Wildfowler Company.

After North American Decoys folded, son Ralf W. Coykendall, Jr. continued a professional career of carving, shifting his talent to producing decoratives. He now lives in Vermont.

PAUL A. SPERRY AND SPERRY DECOYS

Paul Alling Sperry (1895-1982), a native of New Haven, was a versatile businessman, a great sailor, and an entrepreneur. He is best known for inventing the "Sperry Top-Sider" non-skid deck shoe that has gained fame all over the world. He is less well-known as the founder of the ill-fated Sperry Decoy Company.

On returning from World War I, Sperry went into the decoy manufacturing business in New Haven, where he pioneered in producing the first balsa decoys, about 1920. He relied on the American Balsa Company, which had a monopoly on balsa importation, for his raw material. After he had accepted orders from numerous buyers, including Abercrombie and Fitch, the supplier raised the price of balsa. The orders were filled but the business, which was operating on a small profit margin, failed in 1924.

Sperry had a rather extensive line of handsome decoys. They were well constructed, mostly from balsa but also from solid cedar. Excerpts from his advertising brochure are shown.

Two styles of hollow broadbill Barber-like birds found in South Norwalk. Factory made, possibly by Barber Decoys or North American Decoys. Private owner.

A third style (different head) of factory-made broadbill from South Norwalk. Private owner.

BROADBILL CEDAR MODEL

PROFILE GOOSE

"Balsa" (Trade Mark) Model and "Cedar" Model supplied in the following species:

Black Duck	Canvasback
Mallard	Sheldrake
Butterball	Pintail
Green Wing Teal	Redhead
Blue Wing Teal	Broad or Blue Bill
Whistler	Widgeon

"Balsa" (Trade Mark) Chesapeake Model supplied in the following species:

Canvasback	Broad or Blue Bill
Redhead	Whistler

Ducks are packed one dozen in a crate, eight male and four female. The shipping weight of the ducks varies with the specie, "Balsa" (Trade Mark) Model from ten to twenty-two pounds; "Cedar" Model from twenty-five to forty-five pounds.

Geese are made with any length of neck desired, namely, two, three and three and one-half inches. The former is supplied from stock unless otherwise requested. Packed four in a crate.

Brants are packed six in a crate.

Sperry's "Natural" Decoys are for sale by most reliable dealers. If not obtainable at your dealer's, you may procure them direct from the manufacturer.

We try to carry a large stock of all specie on hand, but advise ordering early to avoid delay.

Any model decoy made to order from samples or drawings.

Sold by all reputable Sporting Goods Houses in the United States and Canada.

PAUL A. SPERRY

Manufacturer

Factory: 1033 CAMPBELL AVE., WEST HAVEN, CONN.

Address: P. O. BOX 1153, NEW HAVEN, CONN.

NATURAL SPERRYS DECOYS

NEW-HAVEN — CONN

SPERRY'S NATURAL DECOYS

Made by a Duck Hunter

For a Duck Hunter

THE experienced hunter knows that his success or failure is usually in proportion to the quality of decoys used.

How to "draw" the duck when he is more wary than usual is one of the biggest problems of duck hunting.

This problem has been solved by Sperry's "Natural" Decoys, made and designed by an old duck hunter for the duck hunter.

Sperry's "Natural" Decoys are made to simulate nature as a decoy should [illegible] the sharp vigilant eye of the duck.

Sperry's Decoys are made in two models, the "Balsa" (Trade Mark) Model and the "Cedar" Model. Both are guaranteed to be the best decoys made at their price, and they are warranted to give satisfactory service under the most trying conditions.

SPERRY'S "BALSA" MODEL

Trade Mark

THIS model is made of the well known Balsa wood, one of the lightest materials known, being one-third lighter than cork, and absolutely impervious to water or moisture. It is the same material used in making life-rafts for the U. S. Government.

This decoy is especially adapted for pond shooting, where long "carries" are necessary, eliminating the back breaking labor of long hauling thru the woods that heavy decoys necessitate.

The "Balsa" (Trade Mark) decoy weighs from 12 to 16 ounces. It rides the water like a duck, and does not wallow and roll in rough weather. It rides much higher in the water, making a better showing when only a few decoys are used.

SPERRY'S CEDAR MODEL

SPERRY'S "Cedar" Decoys are declared to be the best decoys on the market at a lower price. It is similar in construction and workmanship to the high grade "Balsa" (Trade Mark) Model."

The "Cedar" Decoy will give long and satisfactory service. It is made only of selected quality cedar, especially treated to resist moisture.

All models are the product of master workmanship. They are coated with a special process "non-glint" paint, and are the only decoys known that will not shine in the sun.

MALLARD "Balsa" (Trade Mark) MODEL

SHELDRAKE "Balsa" (Trade Mark) MODEL

PINTAIL "Balsa" (Trade Mark) MODEL

GREEN WING TEAL "Balsa" (Trade Mark) MODEL

WHISTLER "Balsa" (Trade Mark) MODEL

MALLARD CEDAR MODEL

Sales leaflet from Sperry Decoys.

TUX-DUX DECOYS

Herman Derenthal's Tuxis Wood Products Company, of Madison, Connecticut mass-produced "Tux-Dux" decoys, beginning in the 1930s. They were made with a composite cork body and a wooden bottom board. A simply-designed lathe-turned head was attached by a dowel extending through the body. Low cost was a prime objective and they sold for two dollars apiece. For over 90 percent of the production, a single body shape was made which yielded a maximum number of pieces per unit area of starting material. Though shaped and sized all alike, the painting represented broadbill, black duck, mallard, canvasback and pintail. Some were sold unpainted at a lower price. A few oversized birds of the same construction were made.

In spite of lacking artistic merit, Tux-Dux decoys had the appeal of low cost, and were widely used. They must have been effective; their style was copied along the eastern Connecticut coast by most any gunner who got his hands on old refrigerator insulation. It might be mentioned in this connection that most gunners had a strictly utilitarian interest in decoys, and used whatever material was cheapest, most readily available, or easiest to handle in making them. Several factories sold heads of wood or plastic, which were attached to bodies made or acquired by the gunner. Many garages and basements are cluttered with this type of material.

Other Connecticut manufacturers of the '20s and '30s, of which we have little knowledge, were Brown and Company, West Haven, and Duckoy Manufacturing Company, of Bridgeport.

A TUX-DUX advertisement of Oct. 1939 *Field and Steam.*

TUX-DUX decoys, painted by the user. Private collection.

TUX-DUX black duck. Unused. Private collection.

Bottom of TUX-DUX decoy.

VIII. Shore Birds

The Connecticut coast is rugged, and its beaches are small and scattered. Some of its estuaries and inlets have tidal flats attractive to shore birds, but the great migratory flights of curlews and golden plovers bypassed the state. Other shore birds such as yellowlegs and black-bellied plovers migrated through in smaller numbers than found on Cape Cod and the islands of Massachusetts, Long Island, and the New Jersey shore. There was some gunning of shore birds in Connecticut, but it never gained the prominence attained in these other areas, and as a consequence the number of shore bird decoys found in the State is small.

Hand-carved working shore birds have been found in Stonington, South Norwalk, Saugatuck, Westport, Bridgeport, Stratford, New Haven, Branford, and Essex. Species include yellowlegs, plover, dowitcher, knot, willet, and sandpipers, but few of outstanding quality. Yellowlegs are the most numerous, equalling in number that of all other species combined.

Nearly all of the waterfowl and shore birds killed before the last quarter of the nineteenth century were shot on the water or on the ground with cylinder-bored, muzzle-loading shotguns. Shore birds of this era tend to be heavily peppered with shot, since they sat in the target zone among live birds. As breech-loading guns with choked barrels replaced the older muzzle-loaders in the 1870s, their greater range and accuracy brought about a shift toward wing shooting and shooting for sport. As a result of this change, the later shore birds are generally less shot-riddled. Thus, the number of shot pellets or lack of them in a shore bird can give a clue to, but by no means proof of, its age.

As with duck decoys, but in much smaller numbers, shore birds were made by hunters for their own use. Most were unidentified and will probably never be properly attributed. In this category are the large, slender birds from near Southport by an unknown maker who seemed to follow the same pattern for all species but who varied the shape and length of the bill and the color of the paint to represent different species. Several of these are illustrated. A willet by this maker is shown in Dr. Starr's *Decoys of the Atlantic Flyway,* labelled a Hudsonian curlew.

The earliest Connecticut resident identified as a hunter of shore birds was Captain Nathaniel B. Palmer (1799-1877) of Stonington. He left a string of shore bird decoys, some of which still exist in Stonington. The Palmer shore birds, full-bodied, one-piece (except for bill) yellowlegs and robin snipes, and flat yellowlegs, as well as a strange-looking bird with a turned head, were probably made over a period of about 1820 to 1860. It seems likely that the older-looking, full-bodied birds were made by Nathaniel Palmer. The others may have been later additions by Palmer or even subsequent owners.

Among the oldest shore birds by a known maker are those of Isaac Campbell, of Norwalk, who made plovers and robin snipe, reportedly around 1850. They were hand-whittled with separately made heads. Only lightly sanded, the knife marks are still visible. The were all well painted, and some have baleen bills.

Several other examples of yellowlegs were also found around Norwalk. One skilled craftsman made feeders of three-piece construction with wooden bills. Others less skilled made more conventional birds from single planks, rounded to varying degrees, and with bills of iron wire or nails. One of these was found in what is reputed to be the oldest existing house in Norwalk.

Frank Harlow (1873-1968), a stone mason but a waterman by avocation, made yellowlegs decoys around the turn of the century for use on the mud flats of Branford. His birds were carefully carved, painted in muted tones, and have a lifelike appearance.

A few shore birds came from the Stratford-Bridgeport region. A dowitcher from Stratford and a willet (or yellowlegs) from Bridgeport, both by unknown makers, are shown. Roswell Bliss of Stratford owned a few old yellowlegs at the time of his death. These birds had wire bills and most of them were supported on pairs of heavy wire "legs" to stick in the ground.

Nathaniel Palmer yellowlegs, full-bodied. Stonington Lighthouse Museum.

"Flattie" yellowlegs from rig of Nathaniel Palmer. Stonington Lighthouse Museum.

One of these, a runner, has glass eyes that appear to have been added later, probably by Bliss. Whether he made any working shore birds is unknown, but he did make a few decorative yellowlegs, some with turned-back heads.

The tidal flats on the shores of the islands in the Connecticut River above and below Essex attracted yellowlegs, which in turn attracted the local gunners. Yellowlegs decoys are said to have been made and used here by the famous Essex decoy carver, Sam Collins, Jr., but none have been found to date.

The so-called "lumberyard" birds are reported to have been made in Connecticut, but where and by whom is not known to the writer. They have a characteristic eye groove, a V-separation of wing-tips from tail, and spattered white spots of paint on a black back that identified them as yellowlegs. There may also be other species.

Strange looking shore bird from the Nathaniel Palmer collection. Stonington Lighthouse Museum.

Black-breasted plover by Isaac Campbell of Norwalk c. 1850. Private collection.

Another plover by Isaac Campbell of Norwalk. Private collection.

Knot with baleen bill by Isaac Campbell of Norwalk. Private collection.

Unknown yellowlegs from Westport. Private collection.

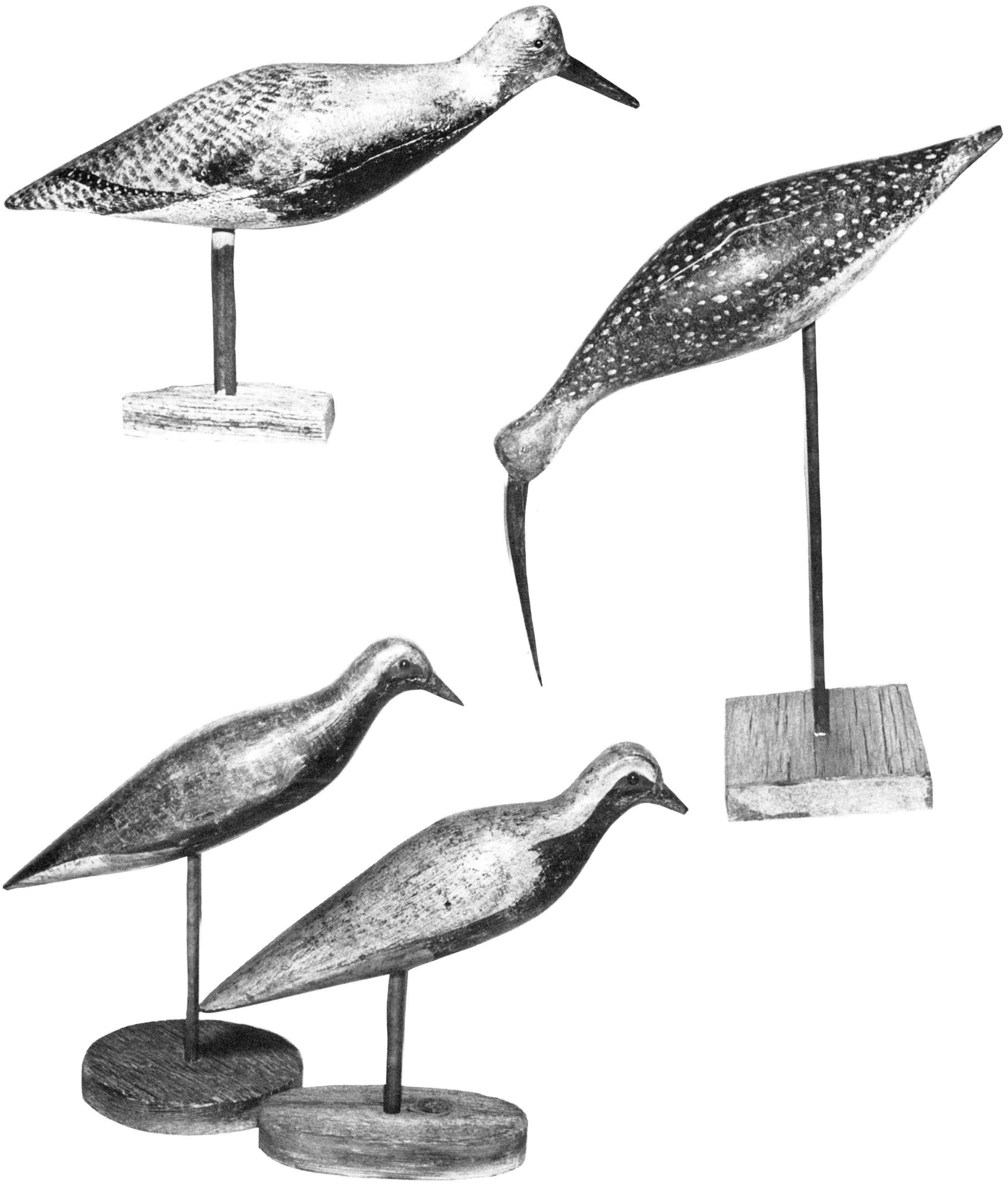

Four decoys from Southport by apparently the same maker. Shelburne Museum.

Unknown Saugatuck yellowlegs. Private collection.

Pair of "flattie" sandpipers from New Haven. Private collection.

Pair of yellowlegs feeders from Norwalk. Private collection.

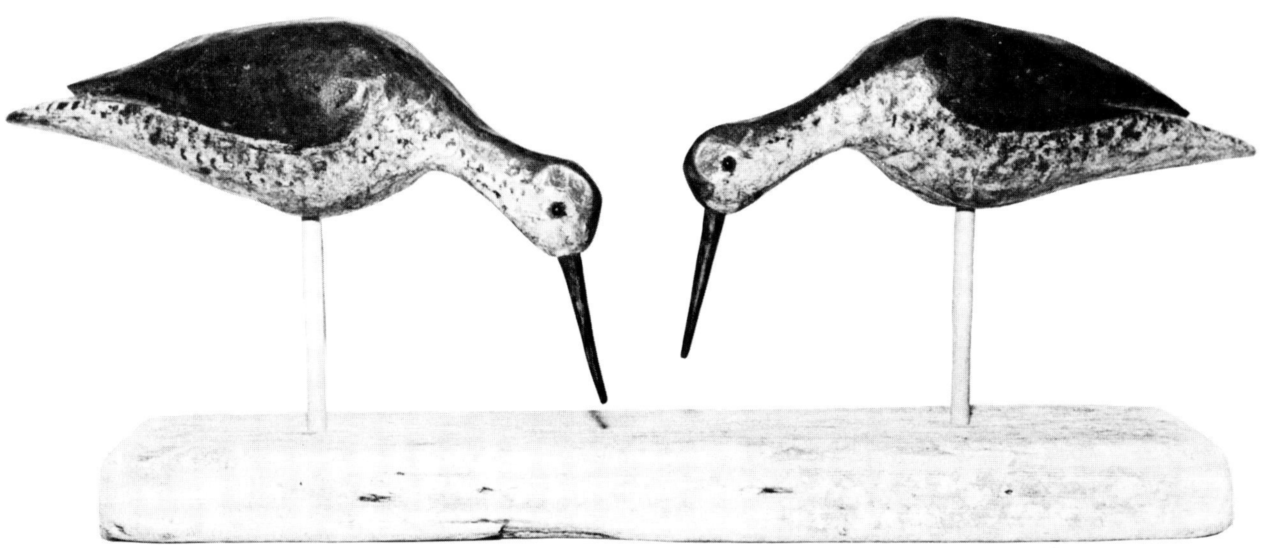

Unknown yellowlegs from Stratford. Private collection.

Dowitcher by unknown Stratford carver. Private collection.

Yellowlegs. Hoffman family, East Haddam, Connecticut. Private collection.

Pair of yellowlegs from Branford. Made by Frank Harlow. Private collection.

Two "Lumberyard" yellowlegs—one full-bodied and the other a "flattie". Private collection.

IX. Descriptive Decoy Features

A. BODY CONSTRUCTION

The first man-made floating decoys used in Connecticut were shaped blocks of solid wood, with heads attached.

When Albert Laing moved to Stratford in 1863, he introduced decoys that had a distinctive shape and were hollow. Being light and more buoyant, they rode the waves more realistically than solid blocks, and their lightness made then easier to transport.

Laing's Stratford associates were quick to adopt his improvements. By the end of the nineteenth century, nearly all of the decoys made in the Housatonic River region were hollow. Strangely, the design did not spread rapidly or far. Except for a few individuals from other locations, who followed patterns given to them by Wheeler in the 1930s or later, the rest of the state clung to solid construction. Hollow working decoys from any other region of the state are uncommon.

The early makers used hand tools exclusively but, from Ben Holmes' time forward, all who produced more than a handful of decoys used a band saw for initial cut of bodies and heads. Patterns were employed, assuring uniformity in size and shape. The rough-cut bodies were rounded with a draw-knife, spoke shave, and rasp, then sanded. For heads, the final shaping was done with wood-carving knives or a pocket knife. Large scale commercial manufacturers used reproducing lathes.

Solid bodies were made from a single block or, less commonly, from two or more boards nailed together. The hollow Stratford decoys followed three general plans of construction: a) with a seam in the middle; top and bottom sections each hollowed by gouge or auger, b) with a seam near the bottom and only the upper section hollowed—the so-called "bottom-board" style of Ben Holmes, and c) box type of three layers, with the middle section hollowed by cutting through, and thin top and bottom sections nailed on. The last type is uncommon even though its method of construction appears to be the easiest. There were variations of these general types, e.g. differences in thickness of the bottom board and in the number of layers.

Seams were caulked with white lead and sections of the body were held together by nails or less commonly by screws, the countersunk holes then filled with putty or wooden plugs. Body parts were frequently glued together after the better waterproof kinds of glue became available. Wheeler, Disbrow, Welles and others made some decoys this way.

A novel method of construction was employed by Fairfield resident Robert Hunter of the Hunter Arms family, who made a body with vertical seams, in contrast to the conventional horizontal seams. Five or six 1" to 1 1/2" boards were laid edgewise and cut roughly to the shape of the body. Centers were cut out by jig-saw from all but the two outer sections, which were to form the sides. The layers were then assembled, glued together, and shaped.

Most Connecticut decoys were made of pine or cedar. At least one very early maker used Philippine mahogany, and some of the last Bliss birds were made wholly or in part of mahogany. In addition to the heavier woods, balsa was used when it became readily available after World War I. Shang Wheeler, Willard Baldwin, and others made a few decoys of balsa. Paul Sperry of New Haven was the first to use it for commercial production of decoys in the early 1920s. Ted Mulliken's Wildfowler factory in Old Saybrook favored balsa. The company also made solid as well as hollow decoys of pine, as described earlier.

Wood continued as the favorite material, but later makers, including Wheeler, also used cork, in the form of natural slab or reconstituted aggregate. When cork aggregate or composite was used, it was often strengthened by a bottom board and an inletted tail, and occasionally with wires running lengthwise through the body. The most highly prized working decoys of Lou Rathmell have cork bodies, but the reason for their acclaim lies in the excellent life-like carving and painting of the heads.

Whatever the body material, the head was carved from wood, commonly sugar pine. Some of the last Bliss decoys with Philippine mahogany bodies also had heads of the same wood. For a while Bliss experimented with cast metal heads which apparently were not very popular, being a little heavy and subject to corrosion, with discoloring and loss of paint.

Heads were attached by a) nails from the top, b) screws or nails up through the top section before assembly of the body, or c) less frequently by dowels. Dowels or metal rods were sometimes used to strengthen necks, for prevention or repair of damage. Dowels were also used by a few early makers to aid in fastening the two sections of the body together. However, by the turn of the century the practice seems to have been abandoned.

The kinds of nails and nailing pattern, and the methods of head attachment characteristic of individual makers, can be used as aids in identification. X-ray photographs are helpful in such examination. X-ray photography is also useful in revealing repairs and especially so in showing head replacement, which appears more commonly than might be suspected. In many cases, reheading cannot be detected by other means.

It has been shown that Laing, in addition to nails, sometimes used a screw from the bottom for regular heads. He used a dowel or peg for other straight heads and all sleepers. Holmes attached heads by two methods, a) the most common, simple nailing from the top using five nails, and b) a single screw from the bottom and two nails from above. He used cut nails throughout in his earlier decoys and wire nails in the later ones. Shang Wheeler attached the heads to his hollow wood decoys in several ways, the commonest being by a single screw or a screw and two nails from the bottom of the upper body section, or by a dowel (as was done for all of his cork and balsa decoys). Cassius Smith and later Kenneth Peck and William Bedell held the head on by two screws from the bottom. Willard Baldwin and most of the other later Stratford carvers used one screw from the bottom, supplemented by two or three nails from below or above to prevent rotation of the head. An excellent but unknown maker whose work closely resembled Holmes' used two wire nails from the bottom, one large and one small.

Dowels or long screws that extended through the body were used for attaching heads to cork-bodied birds. In one known case, with the body constructed from two pieces of composite cork, the head was attached by a screw from the upper half, using a metal plate to back it up, and the lead weight was similarly attached to the bottom half by narrow bolts through a backup plate and held in place by nuts.

Caution must be exercised in drawing conclusions of attribution based on construction, because carvers were great copiers of one another's body shape, nailing technique, and other features of design. Also, some makers, and Wheeler in particular, varied their styles frequently over the years.

Decoys from all of the larger out-of-state manufacturers were used in Connecticut, as were those from the State's own factories of Wildfowler, Paul A. Sperry, and Tux-Dux. Recently, factory decoys with plastic heads, and others made entirely of plastic, paper-mache, rubber, or styrofoam have come into common use and have almost completely replaced the hand-carved birds.

B. BODY WEIGHTS AND ANCHORS

Connecticut decoy weights were almost always of lead. Iron, in the form of ox shoes, railroad spikes, and bolts, found in other areas was seldom used. Some of the weights were simply strips or rectangles cut from lead sheets, at times altered in shape by hammering. Sometimes the lead was inletted by pouring into a key-cut slot in the bottom, in the manner adopted later by New Jersey's Harry V. Shourds. This technique was employed by several makers in Milford, Stratford, and South Norwalk. Inletted lead of an oval shape was most common in the Milford and Branford areas. A few decoys were made to be used without weights, relying on extra width and flat bottoms for stability. Willard Baldwin's earliest birds were of this style.

The preponderance of weights were cast separately and fastened by nails or screws. A variety of different shapes included elliptical, oval, flat bar with rounded ends, ring, and a keel cast around a screw. In the Housatonic region, most of the weights were tapered toward one end and followed the traditional tear drop or pear shape. Within this general "Stratford" type there is a wide variation in width, depth, and size. Ovoid weights were simply molded in a spoon, while other shapes were cast in molds of iron, clay, plaster, or sand, but most often they were made of wood. The biggest problem with wood was charring. With continued use, the resulting product would become increasingly larger and wider. The surface of the weight may sometimes indicate the material of the mold in which it was cast. Occasionally, a definite wood grain can be seen.

One or two holes were drilled in the weight for fastening. The early Stratford weights had only one screw hole. If it was placed away from the center of gravity, minor balance adjustment could be made by rotating the weight slightly. The pointed end of a Holmes weight was often held in place by a small nail or staple. On a few early decoys, the point was inletted to hold it in position. The one-screw weight persisted, but many later makers, including Bliss, Baldwin, and Peck, attached the weight with two screws. A group of Stratford weights are shown on page 189, with provenance as known.

A complete knowledge of weights would aid greatly in the identification of makers and in developing the history of individual decoys. When the original weight is affixed to the bird, the evidence is most helpful, but weights, except for inletted ones, are removable and as a consequence were frequently transferred from one decoy to another. A normal practice in fitting out newly-constructed decoys was to use weights from older worn-out birds. Today, older decoys of a single rig by the same maker are often found with different kinds of weights. Even with these problems, a study of weights can give some clues to the history of a decoy.

Molds and Newly-made Weights

Molds were made by Wheeler and the weights cast by Marshall from a different mold.

Body Weights

First Row:

1. Found on a Laing black duck, stamped "JWS".
2. and 3. B. Holmes original.
4. From an old Milford duck. Point inletted.

Second Row:

1. and 2. Arthur Baldwin decoys.
3., 4., and 5. Shang Wheeler.
6. Early Bliss.
7. Later Bliss.
8. Ken Peck, Bill Bedell.
9. Irving Culver.

Third Row:

1. W. V. Lattin.
2. B. Romer.
3. Early W. C. Baldwin.
4. Later Baldwin.
6. C. Disbrow.
7. C. R. Welles.
8. "Chick" Welles, C. R.'s father.
10. T. C. Marshall.

Fourth Row:

1. From Wheeler-Bliss balsa old squaw.
2. Stamped "J. JONES".
3. Stamped "L F" for Lester Ferris.

Fifth Row:

1. Bliss goose.
6. H. Hoadley.
8. Keel from D. C. Sanford Co., Bridgeport.
9. Copy of the preceding.

ANCHOR WEIGHTS

Most Connecticut anchor weights were made of lead, some with a cast-in wire bail. As elsewhere, nondescript anchors of anything conveniently available, such as heavy fishing sinkers, were used. The commonest type in use in the Stratford area was a lead oval ring on which the anchor line was wound when not in use. The ring was often placed over the head of the decoy for storage. In some cases, the anchor was pierced to receive the line but in most cases it was just tied on.

A collection of decoy anchors used at Stratford is shown on page 189. All are lead except for the fifth one in the last row which is made of iron.

Anchor Weights

First Row:

1. Lou Rathmell.
5. C. R. Welles.

Second Row:

1. D. C. Sanford Co.
2. and 3. R. E. Bliss.
4. Ken Peck.

Fourth Row:

1. and 5. Factory made.
6. Name cast "HOADLY".

All others are unidentified.

Tom Marshall's underwater rig is shown at the bottom of the photograph.

Though decoys were commonly anchored singly, they were sometimes set out in strings of up to a half-dozen, tied one to another. One novel method, apparently unique to Connecticut and used at the New Haven breakwater, was described to me by Tom Marshall. It might be termed an "underwater string," and was designed so that a dog could swim among the decoys without becoming entangled in the connecting lines, which in this case lay on the bottom of the body of water. Three or more decoys were connected to small anchors which were joined by a line from one to the next and finally to a long lead anchor bar. The rig is pictured in the preceding figure.

C. MAKERS AND OWNER'S MARKS

How simple decoy identification would be if all makers and owners had clearly branded or otherwise marked their birds! But they did not. Connecticut decoys were infrequently marked and, when present, a name or initials identified the owner, who might or might not have been the maker. An exception was the Wildfowler trademark brand that was used on many of the decoys sold by the Company. Those sold through sportsmen's supply stores were unbranded.

The best known brand, "LAING," appears on decoys of Albert D. Laing of Stratford. Many of Laing's birds are unbranded and others were branded by their owners. "F. BURRITT" and "B. H. WELLER" are examples. Some of Ben Holmes' birds were imprinted on the bottom with a small "B. HOLMES," about one inch long. Owners' brands appear on Holmes decoys, the commonest being "F. B." and "F. BURRITT" and "A. D. SANFORD" (of Saugatuck). Shang Wheeler did not mark any of his birds except on special occasion, when given to a friend with a note attached to the bottom.

Deeply burned brands "BALDWIN" and "R. BLISS" indicate that the birds were owned by Arthur

Baldwin and Roswell Bliss, respectively. Sometimes both brands are found together, identifying successive owners. Kenneth Peck attributed most of the "BALDWIN" birds to Arthur Baldwin as maker as well as owner about 1890, but is apparent from variation in styles that some were made by others, earlier than Baldwin. In a few cases Baldwin actually burned his "BALDWIN" over "LAING" brands. Some very old decoys from Stratford, apparently made before the influence of Laing became dominant, are branded "S. B. WHEELER." Their owner was Seth B. Wheeler, who ran a hardware store in Stratford in 1870.

Bliss did not brand the birds he made for sale. He did, however, on request, brand birds he had made earlier when they were taken back to him for authentication. Willard C. Baldwin of Stratford did not have a brand until late in his career, when he had two. His first brand was "W C B" in large letters, and his second one the same in smaller letters. He branded only his own work. Some of his later birds, primarily decoratives, were painted by Harold Morse, of New Rochelle, New York. These birds bear the large "W C B" brand and also an "H C M" brand.

Cassius Smith branded his decoys "C. SMITH," and the Smith brothers of Milford carved "S & S" in the bottom.

Brands of later gunners are "T C M" for Tom Marshall, used on a wide variety of decoys he used but did not make, and the monogram "RLH" in a circle, used by Reginald Herring of Essex on birds made by Frank Adams and other carvers of that area.

Some gunners painted or carved their initials on the decoys, rather than using a branding iron. The carved monogram of the letters H and F run together was used by Harry Ferris, a turn-of-the-century Stratford hunter. The letter "W" is carved into decoys found along the coast from Stratford to Branford. A few decoys made by Charles Disbrow have "Disbrow" carved in the bottom, but this may have been done by a later owner to identify the maker. Most Disbrows are unmarked. Horace Merwin of Southport, who copied Wheeler closely, painted his initials "H M" on the bottom of the birds he made.

A few decoys are marked by pressure stamping into the wood. "R P W" in small letters and "W V L" of the same size and spacing are seen on Stratford decoys made about the same time by different men. The former group of letters has not been identified but the latter was used by William V. Lattin, who in one known case spelled out his name completely and added, under the weight, the date "1890." An old black duck that has Holmes characteristics is stamped "R.B.SMITH," the "R" for Radley. He was owner of a hardware store in Stratford around 1900.

Kenneth Peck used letter punches to stamp attributions on a large number of the decoys in his possession shortly before his death.

Names or initials were sometimes stamped into the lead ballast weights. Bliss identified a few of his birds in this manner. Louis Rathmell of Stratford and Danbury used an inletted rectangular weight stamped with his name and date of manufacture. Before Rathmell decoys became highly sought after by collectors, one man is known to have scraped off Rathmell's name, turned the weights over, and sold the Rathmells as "Wheelers."

"J JONES" is found stamped into the inletted weights of old Stratford old squaws. This same name and also "L FERRIS" and "L F," for Lester Ferris, and "H. F." for his brother Henry Ferris, are stamped into the circular washer-shaped weights of decoys of various species used around Stratford about 1900. An old Laing black duck has "J W S" (for J. W. Selleck ?) stamped into the tear-drop weight, and a Cassius Smith whistler is fitted with two small weights, each stamped "F B" (for Francis Burritt). "F W A" is stamped into rectangular weights of Sam Collinses' decoys and others used by Frank Adams of Essex.

The foregoing discussion is concerned with decoys made and used in Connecticut. Mason, Dodge, and other factory decoys were used here and many were branded by the owners. Also, a good many decoys made in Connecticut were used elsewhere, especially in the gunning clubs of Virginia and North Carolina. For example, scaup, redhead, and canvasback decoys made by Ben Holmes were used in a gunning club on Currituck Sound, North Carolina. They are branded "F B A" and, in larger later letters, "W R P" showing successive ownership by club members.

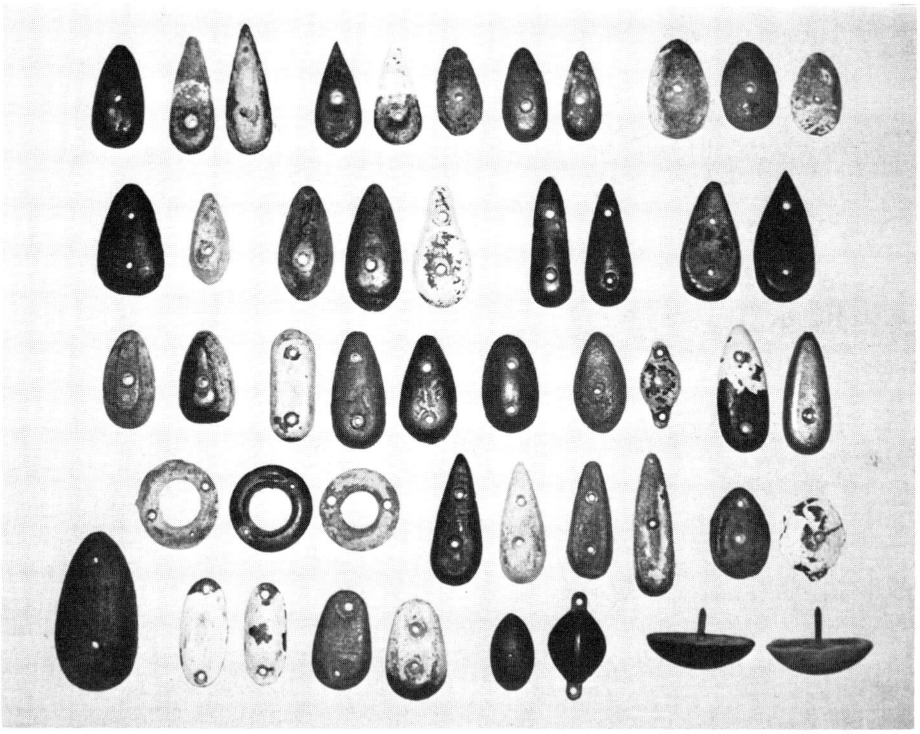

Body weights. (Captions in text).

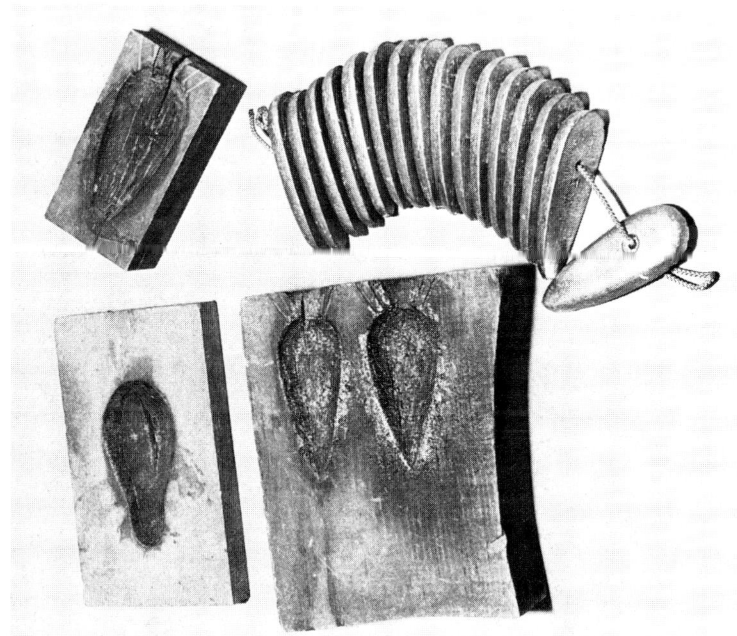

Molds and Weights
Molds made and used by Wheeler. Weights are by Tom Marshall from a different mold.

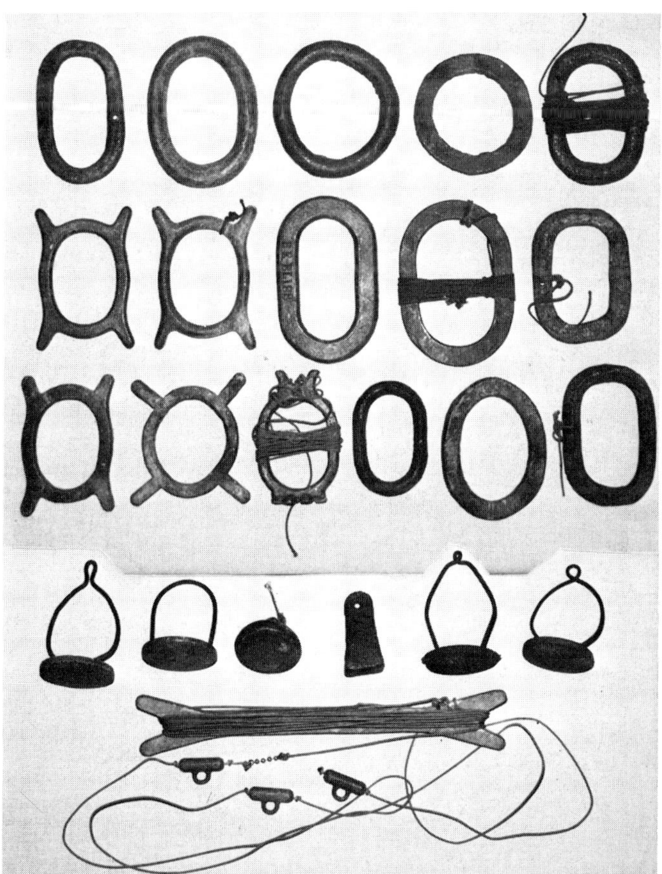

Anchor weights. (Captions in text).

Index

Bold face - Major references
Light face - Ordinary references
Italics - Photographs (65-80 in color), and titles of written works.

All decoys are indexed by maker, if known. Scaup and black ducks and their decoys, because they occur so frequently throughout the book, are not listed by species. Other waterfowl, as well as shore birds, are indexed by both species and maker.